PANCHO VILLA

Recent Titles in Greenwood Biographies

PANCHO VILLA

A Biography

Alejandro Quintana

GREENWOOD BIOGRAPHIES

GREENWOOD

AN IMPRINT OF ABC-CLIO, LLC
Santa Barbara, California • Denver, Colorado • Oxford, England

Library of Congress Cataloging-in-Publication Data

Quintana, Alejandro, 1969–
   Pancho Villa : a biography / Alejandro Quintana.
      p. cm. — (Greenwood biographies)
   Includes bibliographical references and index.
   ISBN 978-0-313-38094-5 (hardcopy : alk. paper) — ISBN 978-0-313-38095-2
(ebook) 1. Villa, Pancho, 1878–1923. 2. Mexico—History—Revolution,
1910–1920. 3. Generals—Mexico—Biography. 4. Revolutionaries—Mexico—
Biography. I. Title.
   F1234.V63Q46 2012
   972.08'16092—dc23 [B]   2011037277

ISBN: 978-0-313-38094-5
EISBN: 978-0-313-38095-2

16 15 14 13 12   1 2 3 4 5

This book is also available on the World Wide Web as an eBook.
Visit www.abc-clio.com for details.

Greenwood
An Imprint of ABC-CLIO, LLC

ABC-CLIO, LLC
130 Cremona Drive, P.O. Box 1911
Santa Barbara, California 93116-1911

This book is printed on acid-free paper ∞

Manufactured in the United States of America

CONTENTS

SERIES FOREWORD

In response to school and library needs, ABC-CLIO publishes this distinguished series of full-length biographies specifically for student use. Prepared by field experts and professionals, these engaging biographies are tailored for students who need challenging yet accessible biographies. Ideal for school assignments and student research, the length, format, and subject areas are designed to meet educators' requirements and students' interests.

ABC-CLIO offers an extensive selection of biographies spanning all curriculum-related subject areas including social studies, the sciences, literature and the arts, history and politics, and popular culture, covering public figures and famous personalities from all time periods and backgrounds, both historic and contemporary, who have made an impact on American and/or world culture. The subjects of these biographies were chosen based on comprehensive feedback from librarians and educators. Consideration was given to both curriculum relevance and inherent interest. Readers will find a wide array of subject choices from fascinating entertainers like Miley Cyrus and Lady Gaga to inspiring leaders like John F. Kennedy and Nelson Mandela, from the greatest athletes of our time like Michael Jordan and Lance Armstrong to the most amazing success stories of our day like J.K. Rowling and Oprah.

While the emphasis is on fact, not glorification, the books are meant to be fun to read. Each volume provides in-depth information about the subject's life from birth through childhood, the teen years, and adulthood. A thorough account relates family background and education, traces personal and professional influences, and explores struggles, accomplishments, and contributions. A timeline highlights the most significant life events against an historical perspective. Bibliographies supplement the reference value of each volume.

PREFACE

Francisco (Pancho) Villa (1878–1923) is certainly one of the best-known personalities of Mexican history, a major leader of the Mexican Revolution (1910–1921). Yet he is often poorly understood. Some admire him as a champion of the poor and weak while others hate him as a bloodthirsty bandit. These contradictory views of Villa are not caused by lack of information. Many books on Villa have been written over the decades. In English one can find early biographies such as *Viva Villa! A Recovery of the Real Pancho Villa* by Edgcumb Pinchon (1934) and more recently *The General and the Jaguar* by Eileen Welsome (2007). In addition, there are a number of films about Villa that go from *Viva Villa!*, starring Wallace Berry (1934), to *And Starring Pancho Villa as Himself* which, despite its title, starred Antonio Banderas (2003). Both views are somewhat accurate. Villa was both a hero and a criminal. He oscillated between these opposite positions due to changing circumstances in extremely violent times. In fact, the accusations that framed him as a bloodthirsty bandit can easily be made about most revolutionary leaders.

Regardless of any opinion that one might have of Villa, whether one sees him as a hero or a bandit, his legacy leaves no doubt of his importance as a revolutionary leader. His role proved so central to the Mexican Revolution that learning about his life is an effective way to understand the many phases of the Mexican Revolution. In the first phase of the revolution (1910–1913), Villa supported General Pascual Orozco's campaign at Ciudad Juarez, the battle that toppled Mexican dictator Porfirio Diaz (1876–1911). During this phase, Villa was also instrumental in the survival of the revolutionary president, Francisco Madero, when the ambitious Orozco turned against Madero. During the second phase of the revolution (1913–1914) Villa became the most successful revolutionary general. He won most of the significant battles that overthrew Mexico's last dictator and President Madero's assassin, General Victoriano Huerta. The third phase was the bloodiest, the result of a split between two revolutionary factions, one led by Villa and the other by Venustiano Carranza. Villa began this phase of the revolution (1914–1915) as the most powerful man in Mexico. However, he failed to transform his enormous regional power into an authentic national movement, a failure resulting in Carranza's victory. Villa spent the fourth phase of the revolution (1916–1921) on the run as an elusive and dangerous rebel. Despite his weak position, he forced the federal government to grant him a generous amnesty as the only way to bring an end to the violence that had haunted Mexico for a decade. Even though the military aspect of the Mexican Revolution is largely considered to have been over when Alvaro Obregon replaced Carranza as president in 1921, Villa's assassination two years later in 1923 resulted from Obregon's concern with Villa's capacity to reignite the revolution during the next presidential campaign. Indeed, Villa's death consolidated the power of Obregon's revolutionary faction.

Villa's apologists and accusers tend to present a simple view of Villa. He appears as either a good leader or an evil bandit. The pro- and anti-Villa propaganda obscures Villa's extraordinary life. He was a fascinating man, capable of overcoming the most difficult odds. He was an illiterate man who became the most powerful man in Mexico, a defeated soldier who managed to evade over 30,000 U.S. and Mexican troops, and he also served as the governor of Chihuahua, creating laws and policies protecting the poor with the support of the wealthy.

Scholars and historians have written several studies on Villa in Spanish and English in the past dozen years. From the biographical point of view, two studies stand out for their efforts to uncover Villa, the man, and eliminate Villa, the myth. These are Friedrich Katz's *The Life and Times of Pancho Villa* (1998) and Paco Ignacio Taibo II's *Pancho Villa* (2006). This book compiles the findings of these and other studies, offering the most current scholarship on Villa available to date. It makes an enormous volume of information manageable and available to high school and college students. Furthermore, this work allows students to have a clearer understanding of the first social revolution of the 20th century.

Portrait of 20th-century Mexican revolutionary leader Pancho Villa. (Library of Congress.)

TIMELINE: EVENTS IN THE LIFE OF PANCHO VILLA

June 5, 1878	Francisco (Pancho) Villa is born Doroteo Arango in San Juan del Rio, in Durango, Mexico.
September 22, 1894	Arango shoots Agustin Lopez Negrete while defending Arango's sister, Martina.
July 10, 1902	Arango moves to Chihuahua to escape Durango's authorities, and changes his name to Francisco (Pancho) Villa.
November 20, 1910	The Mexican Revolution begins.
November 21	Villa attacks the town of San Andres, Chihuahua, his first military action in the revolution.
May 10, 1911	Villa helps Pascual Orozco defeat President Porfirio Diaz in the Battle of Ciudad Juarez.
May 21	Porfirio Diaz resigns as president of Mexico.
October 1	Francisco Madero becomes president of Mexico.
March–August 1912	Orozco rebels against President Madero.
April 2	Villa confronts Orozco at Parral, saving Madero's presidency.

June 3	General Victoriano Huerta arrests Villa and condemns him to the firing squad.
June 4	President Madero changes Villa's death sentence to imprisonment in Mexico City.
December 24–March 6, 1912–1913	Villa escapes prison and moves to Texas.
February 9–18, 1913	General Victoriano Huerta's military coup, later known as the "Ten Tragic Days," results in the assassination of President Madero.
August	Villa becomes the head of the Division of the North.
September 23	Villa achieves his first significant victory against President Victoriano Huerta in the Battle of Torreon.
December 8–January 7, 1913–1914	Villa captures Ciudad Chihuahua, becoming the de facto governor of that state.
February 1914	The "Benton Affair" threatens U.S. support for Villa.
June 25	During the Battle of Zacatecas, Villa destroys President Huerta's last hope to contain the revolution.
October 1–November 5	General Eulalio Gutierrez is appointed president of Mexico by the Convention of Aguascalientes, but the convention fails to unite Venustiano Carranza's and Villa's revolutionary factions.
December 4	Villa meets Emiliano Zapata in the town of Xochimilco, discusses the campaign against Carranza, and takes official control of Mexico City.
January 15, 1915	President Eulalio Gutierrez tries to discharge Villa as leader of the Mexican army; instead Villa forces the president's resignation.
January 28	Carrancista General Alvaro Obregon occupies Mexico City.

April 6–15	Villa's first significant military defeats take place at the First and Second Battles of Celaya.
June 3–5	Villa suffers his third defeat in a row at the hands of General Obregon at the Battle of Leon.
July 8–9	General Obregon effectively destroys Villa's Division of the North during the Battle of Aguascalientes.
October 15	U.S. President Woodrow Wilson officially recognizes Venustiano Carranza as the leader of the revolution.
March 9, 1916	Villa attacks Columbus, New Mexico.
March 15–February 7, 1916–1917	U.S. General John J. Pershing's Punitive Expedition roams the state of Chihuahua but fails to capture Villa.
March 27–July 1, 1917	Villa is hit by a bullet behind his right knee, forcing him to hide in a cave.
January–June 1919	General Felipe Angeles joins Villa in their last serious attempt to overthrow President Carranza.
August 31, 1920	Villa signs an amnesty agreement with the Mexican government, returning to civilian life.
July 23, 1923	Pancho Villa is assassinated in the town of Parral.

Chapter 1

UNDER THE DICTATOR'S BOOT (1876–1910)

During the first three decades of his life (1878–1909), Pancho Villa's world was defined by the rule of a single dictator who directed the fastest modernization process and economic expansion that Mexico had experienced since its independence from Spain in 1821. However, Villa belonged to the vast majority of Mexicans who received little benefit from this prosperity. Instead, people like him experienced the constant threat of poverty and abuse. This dictatorship used the power of the state to prioritize the interests of the wealthy and influential and to keep the vast majority of Mexicans from demanding social justice. For better or for worse, this dictatorship shaped the Mexico in which Villa grew up. It also brought Mexican society to the breaking point that produced the Mexican Revolution. This event transformed Villa, once a humble sharecropper, into possibly the most powerful revolutionary leader in Mexico. Very little is known about Villa's early years, but a lot is known about the Mexico of his youth. A helpful way to understand Villa's reasons for joining the revolution is to understand the nature of the dictatorship that caused the first social revolution of the 20th century.

THE EMERGENCE OF THE DICTATOR

In 1876, two years before Pancho Villa was born, General Porfirio Diaz Mori became president of Mexico. Don Porfirio, as he was commonly known, soon consolidated his power and ruled Mexico as a dictator for several decades. The revolution finally deposed him in 1911, when Villa was 32 years old.

From the very beginning of his presidency Porfirio Diaz showed little interest in using proper democratic procedures to obtain legitimate power. He became president via a military coup, ousting the recently re-elected President Sebastian Lerdo de Tejada. Porfirio Diaz had failed to defeat Lerdo in the ballot box. However, in fairness to Porfirio Diaz, those studying these events should note that some evidence suggests Lerdo became president by rigging that election. Porfirio Diaz, whose campaign emphasized a constitutional ban on presidential re-elections, denounced President Lerdo and used his influence with the military to depose him. Once in power, Diaz reduced the possibility of military coups by co-opting army officers and their 30,000 troops. He did not hesitate to use the army to intimidate his political enemies, especially during his first term in office.[1] As soon as he became president of Mexico, he ignored his anti-reelection slogan and instead managed to gain re-election not once or twice but seven times.

Porfirio Diaz soon consolidated his political base across the country. He systematically replaced elected politicians with his own military and civilian supporters. His appointees were often outsiders to the regions he sent them to administer. Thus, they owed their power directly to him and not to local supporters. Furthermore, Porfirio Diaz seldom used his power to curtail corruption, allowing his appointees to use their offices for personal enrichment. They could, for example, monopolize certain lucrative trades in their respective regions or demand kickbacks from all sorts of government projects. If such politicians managed to develop their own political base, becoming too independent from Porfirio Diaz, the dictator could reappoint them to other regions or ban them completely from politics. In other words, most politicians around the country had much to gain from keeping Porfirio Diaz in power and much to lose by opposing him.

"PAX PORFIRIANA"

Porfirio Diaz's rapid consolidation of power allowed him to bring peace and stability to Mexico, a time later known throughout Mexico as the "Pax Porfiriana," the Peace of Porfirio. For most of the 19th century, Mexico had been subjected to political turmoil, lawlessness, and violence, causing a negative impact on the Mexican economy. Porfirio Diaz was fully aware that a stable Mexico was a prerequisite for prosperity. One of his major accomplishments as dictator was the pacification of Mexico, achieved primarily through coercive means.

Dealing with Bandits

The 19th century offered few economic opportunities to the vast majority of Mexicans, so banditry became one of the few means by which destitute Mexicans could make a decent living. Pancho Villa eventually became one of them. Porfirio Diaz found an interesting solution to this problem. He hired bandits to create a sort of rural police corps. Known as *Rurales*, they proved relatively successful at reducing banditry throughout the countryside. They were easily identified—well armed and well dressed, wearing traditional charro suits. However, the most important weapons used by *Rurales* were intimidation and violence. They fought bandits with few legal limitations. They often terrorized villagers suspected of harboring bandits or demanded food, horses, and other goods. They often acted simultaneously as policemen, judges, and executioners without significant involvement from formal judicial institutions. The *Rurales* often tortured and summarily executed suspected criminals. These draconian practices became an important cornerstone of Porfirio Diaz's "Pax Porfiriana" in the countryside.

The Apache Problem

Banditry had been a historical problem in Mexico, but one of the major threats to Mexico's peace and stability, particularly in Villa's area of northern Mexico, came from a much older problem. Amerindian bands, particularly the Apaches, had threatened villagers since the arrival of the first Spanish settlers. Apache raids in the late 19th century were led by legendary warriors such as Geronimo and Victorio. The Apaches intensified the frequency of their raids in reaction to the encroachment they were suffering from the expansion of U.S. and Mexican towns and increasing settler population. The war against the Apaches often resulted in indiscriminate barbarities committed by all sides: in addition to bloody battles, children were massacred, women were raped, and villages were burned. Both sides wanted to intimidate and drive away the enemy. The result was an exponential increase in violence.

The fight against the Apaches in Chihuahua, Villa's future adopted land, was led by Luis Terrazas. He continued the policy carried out by Spanish colonial authorities of establishing military colonies to protect new settlements, missions, mines, and haciendas. The poor and landless were attracted to these military colonies and joined because military service offered prestige and access to communal lands. The control of these military colonies helped Luis Terrazas become one of the most powerful men in Chihuahua and, eventually, its governor.

This centuries-long war of extermination ended when U.S. soldiers killed Victorio in 1880 and accepted Geronimo's surrender in 1886. As the Apache threat disappeared, the military colonists were no longer needed and, after Terrazas became governor, he promoted new laws to sell the communal lands once used to support these militias. He intended to take advantage of the recently acquired peace and stability by attracting investors to buy land and establish new businesses in the state of Chihuahua. However, seeing the land being taken away from them, many of the military colonists tried to rebel against Terrazas. He managed to keep them under control because the different colonies failed to coordinate their rebellions. Terrazas was able to control the disjointed rebellions and, when needed, he could reinforce his troops by requesting further assistance from the federal government. Thus, Terrazas managed to consolidate his position as a key figure who assisted Porfirio Diaz in modernizing the economy of Chihuahua.

THE ECONOMIC MODERNIZATION OF MEXICO

Porfirio Diaz's success as a dictator was not limited to co-optation of the military and politicians and the coercion of bandits and Apaches. He was a popular dictator, particularly because of the result of his economic policies, and many Mexicans view him as the architect of modern Mexico. Most Mexicans, probably including Villa, were fully aware of the accelerated transformation that the country was experiencing under his leadership. Irrigation works, roads, and ports as well as electricity, telegraph, and railroad lines sprawled throughout the entire country. This not only transformed the landscape with manmade infrastructures, but it also interconnected the country as never before: information, people, and cargo could move easily and rapidly, incorporating previously isolated regions into a truly national economy.

Economic Modernization in Villa's North

Durango and Chihuahua, the states where Villa lived most of his life, benefited from this process. These two states suffered the isolation of regions located far away from Mexico City, the traditional center of political power and economic activity. Thanks to the new advances in communications, Durango and Chihuahua became commercial hubs and major providers of foodstuffs and mineral resources not only to the markets in central Mexico but also to those in the United States.

These expanding markets also transformed the nature of agricultural production in the northern states. Before the arrival of the railroad and telegraph, most rural producers participated in the subsistence economy and sold their products and bought goods in local markets. This satisfied their basic needs and the needs of their communities but did little to expand the regional and national economies. Increased and more efficient access to distant markets dramatically transformed agricultural production into an export economy. This helped attract investors and entrepreneurs to the region. They opened mines, established businesses, or bought large extensions of land (increasingly taken from communities that had worked the land for generations but had no ownership titles) so they could produce a surplus of cattle and grain for exportation.

The Problem with Agricultural Modernization

Porfirio Diaz intensified this trend by passing laws in 1893 and 1894 that established practically no limits to the accumulation of land. The result was that those with more capital were able to buy more land.

These laws produced 6,000 large-scale landowners across the country who held more than 1,000 hectares (2,470 acres); 5 of them owned over a million hectares (2,470,000 acres). These properties were enormous. It took any of these 5 landowners an entire day traveling by train to cross their own property.[2] The result, of course, was that a massive number of people lost their land to a few large-scale landowners. At the beginning of the dictatorship, "it is estimated that approximately forty percent of all land suited for agriculture in the central and southern parts of the county belonged to communal villages. By the end of the dictatorship in 1911, only five percent of that land remained in their hands."[3] The growing number of landless peasants forced to work the land of these vast estates suffered abuse and insufficient compensation.

Regardless of the social implications of this massive redistribution of land, in general the policy was perceived as successful. Many landowners used their vast properties to establish an export-oriented agricultural production that generated large revenues for local, regional, and national governments. The states where Villa grew up, Durango and Chihuahua, became major exporters of products to the United States that included cotton, corn, wheat, oat, beef, milk, silver, gold, lead, zinc, and copper. This increased productivity and flow of capital became an important engine for the Mexican economy that, in turn, brought prestige to Porfirio Diaz's regime.

Foreign Participation in the Mexican Economy

Porfirio Diaz's successful economic policies attracted many European and U.S. financiers and businesspeople to Mexico. In particular, financial capabilities and industrial expertise gave these foreigners an advantage over Mexican businessmen in the highly profitable businesses that required higher initial investment and technological know-how. For example, the French Rothschild and the U.S. Guggenheim families became major investors in the Mexican mining industry. Similarly, U.S. and British investors monopolized the nascent railroad and oil industries. Porfirio Diaz did not show any nationalist concern and instead expressed great interest in attracting even more foreign investment. He secured the passing of legislation that favored foreigners over Mexicans. Foreigners gained the right to acquire property, including subsoil rights, benefits from tax exemptions, and Mexican labor laws more favorable to their interests than the more pro-labor laws of their own countries.

The pro-foreigners policies of Porfirio Diaz produced mixed results. The economic benefits were obvious. Mexico's gross domestic product (GDP) grew eight percent on average every year and in 1896 Mexico managed to pay off its foreign debt for the first time in its history. However, the increased level of foreign control of the Mexican economy also became evident. Many wealthy Mexicans resented that foreigners increasingly controlled major economic activities. Media mogul William Randolph Hearst, who had extensive properties and interests in Mexico, commented at the time: "I really don't see what is to prevent us from owning all of Mexico and running it to suit ourselves."[4] The Mexican upper classes began to find agreement with the concern of the lower classes about Porfirio Diaz's policies. Indeed, a major downside of Porfirio Diaz's economic policies was that economic success was achieved at the cost of a progressive decline of economic opportunities available for Mexicans across all social classes.

MODERNIZATION AND SOCIAL INJUSTICE
Industrial Workers

Porfirio Diaz's policies added substantial burdens to most Mexicans, but particularly the lower classes. Industrial workers became victims of racist discrimination that limited their upper mobility. Administrative and skilled industrial jobs were often occupied by foreigners who had learned their trade back at home. The vast majority of Mexican workers were excluded from proper education and training so they occupied the low-skills positions that only provided meager salaries. This situation, combined with the racist principles of Social Darwinism popular at the time throughout the West, created a false image of the Mexican worker. Mexican workers were stereotyped as too lazy, stupid, and drunk to occupy higher positions in the labor force. Instead of focusing on the need to train and educate them, many industrialists and investors offered high salaries to white foreigners in order attract them to work in Mexico. Mexican workers saw the better working conditions and higher salaries enjoyed by foreigners with jealousy and contempt

and whenever possible they organized strikes to demand similar benefits. Porfirio Diaz, always the champion of peace and stability as a mean
for progress, used the federal army to disband the strikers and send
them back to work.

The Peasants and Small Farmers

Similarly, modernization left a growing number of peasants and small
farmers without land and the export economy made local products
more expensive for them. Facing starvation, an increasing number of
landless peasants were forced to work for the very haciendas that had
taken their lands. Their income was often too low to support their
families so they were forced to request credit from their bosses to buy
basic products that they could only buy in the hacienda's store. These
large landowners, or hacendados, used these debts to force peasants to
work for them under abusive conditions until the debt was fully paid.
The peasants' meager salaries could not allow them to pay their debt,
which created a virtual system of slavery for many Mexican peasants.

Prosperity Coexisting with Misery

The closest that the vast majority of rural workers, including Villa,
could ever get to the prosperity created by Porfirio Diaz's policies was
a distant look at the haciendas' luxurious buildings, fine horses, vast
quantities of cattle, and enormous extensions of land producing abundant cash crops. To add insult to injury, these luxurious houses often
remained empty of people because their owners preferred to live in the
high culture of major cities in Mexico, the United States, or Europe.
They often left their estates under the care of resident managers who
frequently used their authority to abuse peasants and peons. Villa was
one of the peons, observing the luxury that he knew could never be his
while tolerating the abuse of managers.

VILLA'S EARLY YEARS

Pancho Villa was born in the northern state of Durango on June 5,
1878. Very little is known of his prerevolutionary life and many different stories have been written about it without the benefit of much

evidence. Even the circumstances of his birth are not completely clear. Some argue that he was the bastard son of a wealthy hacendado named Don Luis Ferman, who took advantage of his maid, Micaela Arambula, before her wedding night with Agustin Arango.[5] Others argue that Villa's father was indeed Micaela's husband. In either case, Agustin Arango took care of Villa and had four more children with Micaela: Hipolito, Antonio, Mariana, and Martinita. Arango died when Villa was still very young (it is unclear exactly how young). Most likely, Villa was already working helping to support the family before his father died, but Arango's sudden death forced Villa to struggle alongside his mother to support his younger siblings. There is one aspect of Villa's early years on which everybody agrees. His name, "Pancho Villa," perhaps the best known name of the Mexican Revolution, was not his real name. He was born Jose Doroteo Arango Arambula. He changed his name in the late 1890s when he tried to create a new identity while running away from the authorities.

Experiencing the Abuse of Authority

Pancho Villa did not belong to the minority of Mexicans who benefited from Porfirio Diaz's economic boom. In 1894, Villa's life changed unexpectedly and dramatically. The 16-year-old Villa was working in the Hacienda de Gogojito in the state of Durango. The hacienda was administered by Agustin Lopez Negrete and Juan Nepomuceno Flores Manzanera.[6] They used their positions of power to exploit and abuse workers. Villa worked for them as a sharecropper and lived with his family in the workers' quarters of the hacienda.

On September 22, as Villa returned home from the fields, he saw Lopez Negrete trying to take his sister, Martinita (age 15), from the arms of his distressed mother. Outraged, Villa went to his cousin's room and got a gun. He then confronted Lopez Negrete and shot him in the leg. Lopez Negrete's five gunmen entered the room with the intention of killing Villa, but Lopez Negrete cried that he wanted Villa alive. Villa managed to escape, but had nowhere to go. Fearing retribution from Lopez Negrete, few people in the hacienda offered to help him. Villa hid in the mountains while Lopez Negrete patiently waited, believing that sooner or later thirst and hunger would force Villa to return. Without any rush Lopez Negrete decided to go first to the hacienda of Santa Isabel de Berros and take care of his wound. However, Villa showed surprising survival skills and remained in the mountains for several months. Tired of waiting, Lopez Negrete began a manhunt. Eventually Villa was captured, imprisoned, and sent for trial to San Juan del Rio.

In a clear example of the social injustice suffered by poor Mexicans in Porfirio Diaz's Mexico, Villa faced execution by firing squad because he tried to protect his sister. He was desperate. His only hope was to escape. One day the guards ordered him to grind some corn, but, using the metate (grinding stone) as a weapon, Villa attacked them and escaped. He found a horse and rode it to exhaustion. He abandoned the horse and visited a cousin in Rio Grande who fed him and gave him another horse. He spent the next few months, once again, hiding in the mountains.

Forced to Become an Outlaw

While avoiding the authorities, Villa found his options for survival increasingly limited to stealing food. Faced with that reality, he joined two bandits: Ignacio Parra and Refugio Alvarado. To his surprise, he found his life as a bandit quite rewarding. In his first week alone he made 3,000 pesos, 10 times the equivalent of his yearly salary as sharecropper! He devoted a major part of this newly found wealth to the support of his family and also to helping poor people that he encountered on his way. In his mind, helping his family and the poor justified his illegal activities.

Different people draw different conclusions from this period in Villa's life. In the eyes of his supporters, Villa emerged as a local folk hero—a sort of Robin Hood who stole from the wealthy in order to bring some sense of social justice to the poor. In the eyes of his critics, Villa became nothing more than a bloodthirsty bandit. In any event, Villa soon managed to accumulate 50,000 pesos. He then decided to leave the mountains and rejoin his family and friends for as long as the money lasted. Eleven months later he returned to the hills and to his life as a bandit, a double life he lived for several years.[7]

VILLA MOVES TO CHIHUAHUA

By 1902 the situation in Durango grew too dangerous for Villa. His notoriety as a bandit made it increasingly difficult for him to hide and, in addition, he lived in defiance of a conscription order presented to him by the army. As Durango authorities stepped up the manhunt, Villa decided to move to the nearby state of Chihuahua, benefiting from the lack of communication that existed between regional authorities.

Determined to Abandon Banditry

In Chihuahua Villa decided to leave behind his life as a bandit and become a law-abiding citizen. Villa decided to change his identity at this point. Doroteo Arango became Francisco (Pancho) Villa. Villa's father had been the illegitimate son of Jesus Villa and Villa took his new name from this grandfather. He used this new identity to find jobs working for U.S. ranchers and miners, who paid better salaries than their Mexican counterparts. Villa's well-known friendly attitude toward U.S. citizens was perhaps established from this experience. Villa had become a whole new person. He quickly gained the trust of his foreign bosses to move and protect their wealth. On one occasion, he was responsible for the transport of 700,000 pesos for the payroll of mine workers. On another occasion he was responsible for transporting 36 bars of silver and 6 bars of gold. He appreciated the trust vested in him and he claimed that "he never took a cent from these large sums."[8]

THE CHIHUAHUA OF LUIS TERRAZAS

Villa's new life in Chihuahua did not mean that he was above the problems afflicting Mexico. Eventually, he crossed paths with another powerful person who forced him again into illegal activities. His name was Luis Terrazas, the leader of the anti-Apache military colonies.

In Chihuahua, like in most of Mexico, powerful people continued enjoying the use and abuse of power. Terrazas had managed to become the wealthiest and most powerful man in the state, gaining most of his wealth from cattle, mining, and banking. His increasing control over the state's land, laws, and economy allowed him to affect the lives of most people in the state.

The Alliance Between Terrazas and Porfirio Diaz

Before Terrazas could affect the lives of most Chihuahuans, including Pancho Villa, he had to come to terms with the nature of power in

Mexico. As could be expected, the power of the strongman of Chihuahua clashed with the power of Mexico's dictator. Indeed, Terrazas and Porfirio Diaz had a rocky relationship from the very beginning. In 1876 Terrazas supported Sebastian Lerdo de Tejada's candidacy. After his successful coup, Porfirio Diaz replaced the pro-Terrazas governor of Chihuahua with Angel Trias, the political nemesis of Terrazas. Porfirio Diaz's goal, however, was not to eliminate Terrazas, but to dominate the state through a policy of divide and rule. Rather than a direct confrontation, Porfirio Diaz's relationship with Terrazas could better be described as a strategic standoff. Terrazas was willing to limit his political ambitions for Porfirio Diaz's benefit as long as the dictator supported his economic interests. Over time, their political and economic interests grew so intertwined that in 1903 Porfirio Diaz decided to support Luis Terrazas's candidacy for the governorship of Chihuahua. This support helped Terrazas turn the governorship into a quasi dynasty. After his tenure ended, Terrazas was replaced by his son-in-law, Enrique Creel. In due time, Creel was replaced by Terrazas's son, Alberto. This last member of the Terrazas clan was the governor of Chihuahua when the revolution began in 1910.

New Laws Oppressing the People

Between 1905 and 1909 the Terrazas-Creel clan's relationship with the Diaz dictatorship produced such concentration of power that most Chihuahuans began to seriously resent their governors and the dictator who supported them. Policies were drafted to benefit the interest of the clan and its associates, to the detriment of everyone else. In 1905, for example, Terrazas created a new law affecting the use of water and wood, two essential elements for the survival of villagers. Traditionally water and wood were considered the property of the nation so they belonged to no one and everyone. The new law transformed them into commodities that people could own and, therefore, buy and sell. Creeks and hills once accessible to villagers were fenced in by the encroaching haciendas. As it had become the law of the land, villagers daring to challenge this new order were threatened by the hacendados' own militias or Porfirio Diaz's *Rurales*.

Also in 1905, Terrazas issued another new law that allowed hacendados to buy unlimited extensions of land. This further increased the

Pancho Villa (right) and an unidentified soldier during the Mexican Revolution of 1910. (Library of Congress.)

anger of those former members of the military colonies and villagers who continued losing their lands to few wealthy individuals.

THE ECONOMIC CRISIS OF 1906–1909

Adding to the increased pressure the new laws brought on the lower classes, in 1906 an economic crisis hit the country. This was the result of the 1906 financial crises that hit Wall Street. This threw the United States, but also a Mexico increasingly dependent on U.S. investment, into a severe recession that lasted until 1908. Many Mexicans working across the border began returning home when jobs disappeared in the United States. Conditions were not any better in Mexico, and the returnees found only rampant unemployment and misery.

To make matters worse, drought and frost devastated the crops in northern Mexico between 1907 and 1909. Prices of basic products increased together with unemployment. At times fairly and at times unfairly, Chihuahuans of all social classes blamed Terrazas, and his supporter in Mexico City, for their growing misery and despair. The state and federal governments did little to change this impression. Instead of establishing emergency policies to ease the desperate situation of Mexicans, the administrations of Terrazas and Porfirio Diaz used force to suppress the protests of the lower classes.

The Strikes at Rio Blanco and Cananea

In 1907, Jose Ives Limantour, Porfirio Diaz's secretary of finance, applied anti-inflationary policies that shrank the salaries of those lucky enough to have jobs. At the same time, overcapitalization of industrial production forced further layoffs. Porfirio Diaz's administration showed little concern for the suffering of the people. Two strikes became symbols of the growing resentment against the dictatorship. The textile company at Rio Blanco in the state of Veracruz, and the copper mine at Cananea in Sonora, experienced full shutdowns caused by striking workers demanding better living and working conditions. The workers refused to submit to threats by the companies' administrations and by the government. Porfirio Diaz sent federal soldiers to force the workers back to work. The workers continued to resist, and the situation in Rio Blanco and Cananea escalated into an open confrontation. In a few hours, somewhere between 50 and 70 workers were killed in each place. Porfirio Diaz showed no remorse. The benevolent dictator, the architect of modern Mexico, now was perceived as a tyrant willing to spill the blood of hard-working Mexicans in order to protect the investment of foreigners.

Another confrontation, this time between Porfirio Diaz's government and Yaqui Indians, in the state of Sonora confirmed such feelings. The U.S.-owned Richardson Construction Company was trying to buy from the Mexican government communal lands the Yaqui claimed had belonged to them since ancestral times. Hundreds of Yaquis were killed as they resisted the army that tried to remove them from their land. Many more were captured, placed in trains, and sent to the opposite side of the country. In the state of Yucatan they were forced to work in hemp plantations, far away from their families, lands, and traditions, in conditions that constituted slavery. For Porfirio Diaz this was a great solution. He solved the land conflict in Sonora and satisfied the labor needs of the rapidly expanding hemp industry in Yucatan. For the Yaquis it was a death sentence. Thousands died in Yucatan of either despair or overwork.

VILLA CONFRONTED BY TERRAZAS

Pancho Villa arrived in Chihuahua shortly before Terrazas became governor and before the economic crisis began. After having worked as a freelancer for several employers, he settled down in the town of Parral where he hoped to establish his own business buying and selling meat. This brought Villa in contact with Terrazas. Villa was unaware that the Terrazas-Creel clan monopolized the meat industry in Chihuahua. The clan did not allow independent sellers so it blocked Villa's meat providers. In order to maintain his business Villa decided to become a cattle rustler, but that did not necessarily mean that Villa was returning to illegal activities. Rustling was part of an ancient tradition in northern Mexico. All unmarked cattle roaming freely had no official owner, so Villa rightly considered this a legitimate way to provide for his own butcher shop. However, just as Luis Terrazas had done with water and wood, he ended a centuries-long tradition by enacting another law making cattle the private property of the landowner where cattle were found. Given the massive extension of land owned by hacendados, this law practically equated rustling with stealing from hacendados.

THE LOOMING REVOLUTION

Villa was frustrated. He was trying his best to stay within the limits of the law, but believed he was being forced once again to become an outlaw. Unemployment began to make matters worse for most Mexicans, and resentment against the regime was at an all-time high. This made Mexicans increasingly susceptible to the revolutionary rhetoric that started to spread throughout the country. A variety of political groups began to denounce the abuse of power experienced under the regimes of Terrazas and Porfirio Diaz, and many decided to join multi-class political movements to challenge these regimes. At this point Villa was apolitical but circumstances drew him into the revolution that made him one of the best known figures in Mexican history.

NOTES

1. Cosio Villegas, *Historia General de Mexico* (Mexico: El Colegio de Mexico, 2009), 660.

2. Luis Gonzales, in *Historia General de Mexico*, Cosio Villegas, ed. (Mexico: El Colegio de Mexico, 2009), 682.

3. Friedrich Katz, *Mexico since Independence*, Leslie Bethell, ed. (New York: Oxford University Press, 1999), 94.

4. Michael J. Gonzales, *The Mexican Revolution, 1910–1940* (Albuquerque: The University of New Mexico Press, 2002), 9.

5. Robert L. Scheina, *Villa: Soldier of the Mexican Revolution* (Dulles, VA: Potomac Books, 2004), 4.

6. Guadalupe Villa and Rosa Helia Villa, eds., *Pancho Villa: Retrato Autobiográfico, 1894–1914* (Mexico, DF: Santillana Ediciones Generales, 2005), 79.

7. Friedrich Katz, *The Life and Times of Pancho Villa* (Stanford, CA: Stanford University Press, 1998), 66.

8. Ibid., 69.

Chapter 2

VILLA AND THE APOSTLE
OF DEMOCRACY (1910–1913)

It turned out to be a momentous event when Pancho Villa decided to reinvent himself by moving to the state of Chihuahua. Partly due to the abusive policies of the Terrazas-Creel clan, sometime after arriving in Chihuahua, Villa experienced a rapid social and political radicalization. He had left Durango resentful of the exploitative practices of hacendados and the use of the levy to force him to join the army. He looked for better living conditions in Chihuahua, but after a brief period of financial success, Chihuahua proved no better. Villa's plan to establish a butcher shop was frustrated by the Terrazas-Creel meat monopoly. Regardless of his best efforts to the contrary, he was forced once again to operate outside of the law. He felt abused and identified with other people being exploited in Chihuahua: hacienda peons, industrial workers, miners, and the residents of military villages. Eventually, Villa became receptive to the radical rhetoric spreading throughout the state calling for the violent overthrow of Porfirio Diaz.

However, even radicalized regions like Chihuahua needed a leader willing to confront Porfirio Diaz. Ironically, the leader who stepped forward was not a proven military leader or a charismatic figure emerging from the oppressed masses. In 1909, Francisco Madero, a physically unimpressive man and wealthy hacendado, emerged as the unlikely leader of the revolution. He was, however, a leader determined to confront the mighty Porfirio Diaz. Radicalized Chihuahuans, including Pancho Villa, soon demonstrated their willingness to fight for Madero. By so doing, Villa sealed his fate. He soon became one of the most charismatic and effective leaders of the Mexican Revolution and eventually one of the best known heroes in Mexican history.

PORFIRIO DIAZ'S "DEMOCRACY"

Before Madero could ignite the revolution that would transform Villa's life, circumstances had to bring the country to a breaking point in order for the upper and lower classes in Mexico to unite against Porfirio Diaz. The lower classes needed no such additional incentive, but the radicalization of the upper classes was stimulated, in part, by an offhand comment made by Porfirio Diaz. In 1908 the dictator carelessly declared to U.S. journalist James Creelman that Mexico was ready for democracy and promised not to seek re-election. This comment inspired a complete mobilization of middle- and upper-class citizens seeking an opportunity in politics. Many young professionals jumped at the possibility of replacing Porfirio Diaz and his aging political cronies. Many of them, including Francisco Madero, began to organize political parties in preparation for the 1910 general election. Madero became the presidential candidate of the Anti-Reelectionist Party. However, as everybody prepared for the end of the dictatorship, Porfirio Diaz had a change of heart and announced his candidacy for the presidency. The initial excitement experienced by the upper classes turned into anger. Many new political parties committed themselves to opposing Porfirio Diaz's attempt to remain in power.

The activism against Porfirio Diaz's candidacy united multi-class groups behind Madero's message. Madero stood with the most outspoken politicians who publically demanded that Porfirio Diaz honor his old political promises. During his first run for the presidency in 1876, Porfirio Diaz had challenged President Lerdo de Tejada with his own anti-reelectionist slogan. The dictator dismissed Madero, considering him of no consequence, and continued with his plan to remain in power. Contrary to Porfirio Diaz's expectation, Madero's message was widely accepted across Mexico.

Madero's Presidential Campaign

Madero did not give up his determination to become president of Mexico after Porfirio Diaz made clear his determination to remain in power. After all, it appeared he had a chance of winning. Madero's political rallies attracted large numbers of supporters fed up with the status quo. He forcibly denounced Porfirio Diaz's failure to keep his promise of democracy and reminded his supporters that the dictator had manipulated elections in order to remain in power. To Porfirio Diaz's surprise, Madero enjoyed far more support than he had expected.

Madero became a significant threat to Diaz's re-election. The seriousness of this threat was in part due to Madero's wide appeal. His anti-dictatorship rhetoric appealed to the radicalized masses, while his family pedigree and social status appealed to the most conservative upper classes ready for change but afraid of the chaos and anarchy that might result from more radical changes advocated by others. His message of democracy and the end of the dictatorship was sensible enough and appealed to the vast majority of Mexicans.

Due to his growing popularity, Madero began to suffer constant harassment by the authorities. He was not easily intimidated and showed determination to continue challenging the dictatorship. Porfirio Diaz finally ordered Madero's arrest in preparation for election day. From his prison cell in San Luis Potosi, Madero learned the outrageous result of the election; officially, he received 200 votes while Porfirio Diaz received over one million. The size of Madero's rallies and the widespread support he had enjoyed throughout the country during the months leading up to the election left no doubt to most Mexicans that the results were ludicrous. Madero's supporters around the country refused to concede and began contemplating violent resistance.

THE BEGINNINGS OF THE
MEXICAN REVOLUTION
The Plan of San Luis (1910)

While still in prison at San Luis Potosi, Madero wrote a plan that declared Porfirio Diaz's re-election illegitimate. The "Plan of San Luis" also outlined policies aimed at solving serious social problems afflicting the nation, including land reform, better working conditions, the consolidation of democracy, and the end of crony politics. The plan concluded that all this could be achieved only after the violent over-throw of Porfirio Diaz.

Madero managed to escape to San Antonio, Texas, where he made his plan public. He gave Porfirio Diaz until November 20, 1910 to step down. If he refused, Madero would call on his supporters to begin hostilities against the illegitimate regime.

Villa Joins Madero's Movement

Pancho Villa was not an activist politician but was attracted by Madero's antiestablishment rhetoric. He very likely kept a limited interest in politics during the presidential campaigns. He probably began to pay close attention to political developments only after the publication of the Plan of San Luis. Indeed, the plan attracted the attention of vast numbers of Mexicans from all classes and political orientations.

Villa and most Chihuahuans saw Madero's movement as an opportunity to get rid of the Terrazas-Creel clan in Chihuahua. Villa began to entertain the possibility of joining the revolution when he was approached by Abraham Gonzalez, a Maderista leader in Chihuahua. Gonzalez knew Villa from the cattle business.[1] He convinced him that Madero's call to arms would free Chihuahua from its own dictatorship. Villa saw a direct and clear benefit in Madero's movement and agreed to join the revolution.

It is unclear why Gonzalez decided to invite Villa to join Madero. Villa, after all, had no real political or military experience and his past as a bandit could be a liability. Madero was interested in keeping his revolution within the legality of the constitution. After all, he had accused Porfirio Diaz of breaking an anti-reelectionist law. Manning his revolution with bandits could delegitimize his movement, as it give the impression that his movement was nothing more than an invitation to bring looting and chaos to the country. As a norm Madero refused to incorporate bandits into his movement. For this reason, it is surprising that Villa, a somewhat well-known outlaw, was invited to form part of Madero's revolution. It is possible, however, that Gonzalez was interested in Villa's well-known talents: his remarkable horsemanship, detailed knowledge of the countryside, superb use of his gun, and the capacity for controlling his men. In any event, Gonzalez was responsible for convincing Villa to join the revolution. Villa accepted and joined the revolution as the second-in-command leader of a twenty-eight-member gang of former cattle rustlers under the command of Castulo Herrera.[2]

The Beginning of Hostilities

Madero began making preparations to initiate hostilities against the dictatorship, but Porfirio Diaz was not particularly worried about the threat. He remained convinced that he could easily nip the revolution in the bud, as he had done with previous rebellions. In the beginning, things looked promising for the old dictator. On November 13, federal forces discovered a conspiracy in Cuchillo Parado, Chihuahua. The leader of the village, Toribio Ortega, decided that waiting for the November 20 deadline was too dangerous. The next day he took his 60 men and attacked the town's garrison. This was the first confrontation of the revolution. Ortega forced Ezequiel Montiel, the local political representative of the Terrazas administration, to flee town. However, this spark failed to ignite a nationwide revolution, and peace and quite returned to the country. On November 18, authorities uncovered another of Madero's supporters at the city of Puebla in central Mexico. The police stormed the house of the local Maderista leader upon discovering its use as a weapons depot. The owner, Aquiles Serdan, was killed during the attack and many of his supporters were either killed or captured. The confrontation between these Maderistas and the police also failed to ignite the revolution. Many people began to doubt that Madero's movement was popular enough to spread widely throughout the country, which was a precondition for successfully deposing the old dictator. As long as Porfirio Diaz could concentrate his military power to suppress specific points of rebellion, he had no problem controlling the uprising. Porfirio Diaz was confident that he would succeed, because November 20, the deadline set by Madero, was a relatively quiet day that saw only a few skirmishes, particularly in Chihuahua, but nothing more. The revolution appeared to have misfired.

Villa's First Revolutionary Activities

Pancho Villa's and Castulo Herrera's small gang of cattle rustlers boasted some of the few Maderistas across the country with enough courage to attack the federal army without waiting for a widespread uprising. Many revolutionaries were concerned that once they began fighting few would follow, leaving them vulnerable to the federal army, but not Villa and his men. On November 21, they occupied the town of San Andres. That same day, federal troops were sent to retake the town. Villa refused to withdraw and decided to surprise the army by attacking them as they stepped off the train at San Andres's railway station. One of the first casualties during this attack was Captain Yepez, the federal commanding officer. The loss of leadership caused confusion and resulted in a retreat by the federal troops.[3]

Within the larger scope of the Mexican Revolution, Villa's first skirmish was relatively insignificant. However, even at this early stage of the revolution, Villa exhibited certain characteristics that contributed to his meteoric rise within the ranks of the revolution. First, he demonstrated that a small group of untrained men could defeat the federal army by avoiding a direct confrontation and using surprise attacks. Second, he demonstrated the importance of keeping his men under control. The inhabitants of San Andres were terrified when they saw their town invaded by a horde of revolutionaries. As they braced themselves for the expected looting and chaos, they saw with surprise that Villa kept his men under discipline, bringing instead a sense of security to the village. In addition, Villa demonstrated his natural charisma and leadership. In fact, during these attacks, Villa, not Castulo Herrera, orchestrated and led the attacks on the garrison and the train station.[4]

Perhaps even more important to the eventual success of the revolution, Villa's charisma attracted more people to the cause of the revolution. His first skirmish convinced hundreds of peons and peasants in Chihuahua that a revolutionary victory was possible, so they decided to join the movement. Obviously, his own group benefited, and his gang began to grow quite rapidly. By the second half of November Villa's militia had grown from 24 to about 325 men. By early December he could count close to 500 revolutionaries under his command. This was a huge personal accomplishment. At this point Villa was not considered a particularly important leader of the Maderista movement. Yet, in only one month, his group already provided about ⅓ of the 1,500 revolutionary soldiers fighting in the state of Chihuahua.

Villa's popularity continued growing together with that of the revolution. Stories of his ingenious sneak attacks were told and retold throughout the state. For example, in early December, Castulo Herrera and Villa led their 500 men in an attack on Ciudad Chihuahua, the capital of the state—a major target most revolutionaries did not dare approach. As they moved toward the city, Villa led a reconnaissance expedition of 40 men. He spotted 700 federal troops scouting the area and unwisely tried to engage them. Villa and his men soon recognized that they were about to be trapped in a gorge. In order to avoid capture, they managed to place a large number of sombreros in the surrounding hills, making the federal soldiers believe that they were fighting a larger force, which forced the federals to move cautiously while Villa and his men escaped unscathed.[5] It was this ingenuity that made Villa a popular hero and a successful leader. People noticed that, regardless of the federal army's military superiority, Villa was able to mock them and get away with it. People loved the stories and continued joining his military force.

MADERO'S EFFORTS TO LEAD THE REVOLUTION

Despite Villa's successful skirmishes and rising popularity, the revolutionary leadership did not appear capable of transforming those random attacks on the federal army into a truly united revolutionary movement at the national level. Madero had inspired the movement but he had failed to transform himself into its leader. He was eager to command the revolution but could not because he still lived in exile due to an arrest warrant. Not surprisingly, very few would-be revolutionaries were willing to risk their lives for someone enjoying safe haven in the United States. Madero understood that the success of the revolution depended on his ability to return to Mexico and unite all the disparate rebellions sprouting throughout the country. He was eager to do so but he first needed a gateway controlled by the revolution that he could use to enter Mexico.

Madero's Complicated Return to Mexico

The leader in exile needed to find safe access to Mexico. Chihuahua was the most obvious alternative for Madero's return, but it was not his first choice. Chihuahua was certainly the border state with the largest number of armed rebels willing to confront the federal army, but Madero remained unsure. Most of the leaders in the state had lost connection with his party and some mistrusted him because of his background as a wealthy landowner. At this point, the most important military leader of the revolution in Chihuahua was Pascual Orozco (Villa was still only a promising rising star). Orozco harbored his own political ambitions and his loyalty to Madero was fragile at best. In addition, most revolutionary forces were nothing more than a motley group of people led by ambitious local leaders focused on using the revolution to advance their own political interests. Many of them had no interest in Madero's national agenda. These leaders were primarily interested in the elimination of the Terrazas-Creel clan, the real threat to their local ambitions.

Madero simply did not feel that he could trust all the revolutionary leaders in Chihuahua. Chihuahua's military leaders not only retained questionable loyalty to Madero, the area's revolutionary ideologues did not particularly admire him. Intellectually, Chihuahua's revolution was influenced more by the radical anarcho-syndicalism of the Flores Magon brothers than by Madero's democratic reforms. The Flores Magon brothers considered Madero a bourgeois solely interested in political palliatives and not in a true revolutionary transformation of Mexico's political and social realities. They believed that they could lead the real revolution and did not need Madero's help.

Even Pancho Villa had some reservations about Madero's goals. Villa's reasons were less political or ideological. He simply wanted to help Chihuahuans get rid of the Terrazas-Creel clan in order to facilitate social justice and economic opportunities for all. He felt unsure about Madero's intentions. Like most poor Mexicans, he remained suspicious of any rich man claiming to represent the interests of the poor. As far as Villa was concerned, Madero needed to demonstrate his commitment to the revolution by fighting hand-in-hand with the rest of the revolutionaries. He was willing to help Madero re-enter Mexico and prove himself, but Madero preferred to explore other alternatives.

Regardless of his concerns, Madero had practically no other alternative but to enter Mexico via Chihuahua. He explored other alternatives. First, he considered his home state of Coahuila, also a border state. There, he enjoyed the complete trust of most of the revolutionary leadership. After all, some of the most important revolutionary leaders of Coahuila were members of his own family or close family friends. His second option was to sail from New Orleans to the port of Veracruz in the Gulf of Mexico, where he also enjoyed strong support. But neither Coahuila nor Veracruz had enough military strength to guarantee his safety.

In early February 1911, Madero finally decided to enter Mexico through Chihuahua. This decision brought Villa in direct contact with Madero and facilitated his transformation into a key figure of the revolution.

Madero Returns to Mexico

Madero chose to use Ciudad Juarez, Chihuahua, as his port of entry and ordered Orozco to occupy the city. For Madero the city represented more than an entry to Mexico. The city was divided from El Paso, Texas only by the Rio Grande. These sister cities could allow the safe establishment of his revolutionary government as money and arms could be easily smuggled from the United States. In addition, it offered direct diplomatic connections with the U.S. government, essential for the success of his movement. This city was also a major commercial hub and could offer additional income by appropriating the custom offices and collecting import and export taxes. In case of a dangerous advancement of federal forces against the revolution, this city could also offer an emergency exit into the United States.

Unfortunately for Madero, Orozco considered unrealistic the possibility of occupying Ciudad Juarez. Up to now, the revolutionaries had been able to fool the army only in sneak attacks and isolated skirmishes, but they had never encountered the better armed and trained federal army in a head-on confrontation. Orozco made his concerns known to Madero. On February 14, 1911, Madero decided not to wait any longer and sneaked into Mexico to join Orozco's camp in Chihuahua.

Madero's Fiasco as Military Leader

Even after Madero joined his forces, Orozco continued expressing his doubts about the possibility of capturing the border town. Madero, however, remained determined. He decided to personally lead the attack on Ciudad Juarez and jump-start the revolution. His determination and willingness to get involved in military action impressed Villa and his men. However, regardless of his enthusiasm, Madero's first military action of his life was a dismal failure. He did not attack Ciudad Juarez. He realized that Orozco was right and decided to first try an easier target. Indeed, even the nearby town of Casas Grandes proved too much for the limited firepower of his revolutionary forces. Porfirio Diaz had been fairly unconcerned about most of the skirmishes but paid special attention to Madero's first military action. The easy victory of the federal forces convinced Porfirio Diaz that this defeat had destroyed the insurrection. He now expected the prompt return of peace and order to the country.

THE REVOLUTION'S UNEXPECTED SUCCESS

To the surprise of everyone, Madero's first military blunder produced the opposite effect that Porfirio Diaz, and most Mexicans, had expected. The battle at Casas Grandes was not the last nail in the revolution's coffin. Instead, this battle allowed most revolutionary leaders to respect Madero for his courage and commitment to the revolution. Madero fought hand-in-hand with his troops, thus putting his own life at risk. Villa was very impressed and from then on he respected Madero's leadership. The battle at Casas Grandes convinced many more to support the leader of the revolution.

Dictatorship in Trouble

After the battle at Casas Grandes, Madero's movement began spreading throughout Mexico. More and more people believed in the possibility of ending the three-decades-long dictatorship. By late February 1911, other rebel groups began confronting the federal army in all corners of the country. Porfirio Diaz's army was rapidly overwhelmed by the number of outbreaks. The army had been very effective at mobilizing forces and eliminating sporadic uprisings and rebellions, but it was ill prepared for a general national insurrection on numerous fronts.

Porfirio Diaz needed to increase the numbers of troops to resist the revolutionary challenge. He used the traditional method to enlist soldiers, the levy—the forced conscription of poor Mexicans. Traditionally, those forced to join the federal army had no way out. If they did not respond to the call, they faced imprisonment and severe economic penalties that could cause the ruin and starvation of their families. However, things were very different now. Some who were not interested in joining the army could flee their towns and join the revolution. In other words, Porfirio Diaz's effort to strengthen his army became another reason for the increase of the strength of revolutionary forces.

The tide was now on Madero's side. Even the wealthy landowners began supporting the revolution. They had traditionally used their workers as militiamen to support the government and control rebels in their localities. Now, the government was incapable of containing this growing rebellion and many landowners began to believe that the government could no longer protect them. They felt that supporting the government made them vulnerable to rebel attacks. Instead of fighting on behalf of the government and risking looting and possibly death, many landowners decided to donate their cattle and water to feed the rebels and used their workers to fight with the revolution, not against it. Porfirio Diaz's supporting militias used to contain rebellions disintegrated.

Furthermore, Villa and other revolutionaries figured out a weak point in Porfirio Diaz's military tactics. Destroying train tracks and telegraph lines seriously reduced the capacity of the federal government to oppose the insurrection. The government used railroads to quickly move large numbers of troops and resources wherever they were needed. Similarly, the telegraph was indispensable to the federal army for gathering information and expediting the delivery of orders, as well as determining proper strategies and coordinating attacks. The once mighty federal army was becoming a weak and uncoordinated enemy.

At this moment of the revolution, Villa was recognized as one of the most successful guerrilla fighters. His successful skirmishes and brief encounters with federal troops had inspired many others to follow his strategy. No formal revolutionary army existed, but hundreds of leaders like Villa overwhelmed the federal army.

For the first time, Porfirio Diaz seriously considered negotiations with Madero. He could either escalate the war or try to find a peaceful solution. He was concerned that a prolonged war would destroy the Mexican economy and its infrastructure, two of his most important legacies. He promised to address their grievances if the revolutionaries put down their weapons. Once again, his plan backfired. Many revolutionaries considered Porfirio Diaz an uncompromising dictator. The fact that he was willing to negotiate suggested that they had managed to break the regime, and they felt emboldened. Instead of negotiating, many preferred to continue fighting. Total victory was the best way to guarantee the goals of the revolution. Madero now considered attacking Ciudad Juarez to deliver the final blow to the dictatorship.

VILLA'S KEY ROLE IN MADERO'S VICTORY

The campaign to take Ciudad Juarez was a major step forward in transforming Pancho Villa into a major player of the revolution. As discussed earlier, Madero had found it difficult to gain the trust of several Chihuahuan revolutionaries. Villa suddenly emerged as the best alternative available for Madero to gain control of the political situation in Chihuahua. Villa very quickly became Madero's confidante and, therefore, a key figure of the revolution.

Madero's Growing Political Difficulties in Chihuahua

Madero understood that his position as leader of the revolution depended on leading a major and significant victory at Ciudad Juarez. By early March 1911, his forces were much stronger and the federal army looked weaker than they had the previous month. However, before launching such an important attack, Madero needed to make sure that he had the effective command of the revolutionary forces in Chihuahua. In particular, Madero needed to assert his authority over the Flores Magon brothers and their numerous anarchist supporters—the Magonistas. This group was determined to take the revolutionary leadership from Madero in order to lead a more radical movement. Madero considered using Pascual Orozco, still the most accomplished military leader of the revolution, to help him tame the Magonistas. However, Orozco's political interests benefited from the division. He was interested in playing the role of mediator to increase his political clout. When Madero ordered Orozco to disarm the Magonistas, he refused, believing that Madero was completely dependent on him. However, Orozco did not take into account that Madero had an alternative to help him bring the Magonistas under control: Pancho Villa.

Villa's Growing Strength

At this time, Villa directly commanded some 700 troops and was already emerging as one of the most important military leaders of the revolution, perhaps second only to Orozco. Regardless of his lack of education and formal military training, Villa enjoyed enormous support among the increasing number of people under his command. He still had no significant victories under his belt, but he had demonstrated countless times that he was a courageous commander, willing to fight side-by-side with his soldiers during every confrontation against the federal troops. He also had shown a great talent for planning sneak attacks that, while unable to destroy the enemy, exposed the vulnerabilities of the federal forces and delighted revolutionary sympathizers.

Villa's army was one of the most popular and fastest growing of the revolution. This was due also to his tactics that often resulted in a minimal number of casualties among his men. In addition, Villa always made sure to keep his troops well fed, well paid, and well armed. Usually, Villa raided haciendas and used their cattle and other resources to satisfy the needs of his troops. However, his raids were always carefully calculated. He limited his attacks to hated wealthy hacendados, so as not to upset the general population. In fact, his army was already being recognized as one of the most disciplined of the revolution. Unlike most military forces, including the federal army, he continued to make certain that his troops did not appear as violent barbarians looting and destroying everything in their path. He respected and protected the interests of villagers and, particularly, those of American hacendados—perhaps this was due to the fair treatment that he received while working for them during his first years in Chihuahua. This provided Villa with important supporters on both sides of the Mexican border.

Villa Saves Madero

Villa's growing strength did not pass unnoticed and Madero made the fateful decision of asking Villa to help him control Chihuahuan revolutionaries. Villa's effectiveness impressed Madero. He proved more than capable of neutralizing the Magonistas without disrupting the cohesiveness of the revolution. He understood that he could not simply begin shooting at the Magonistas. After all, they were fellow revolutionaries. Instead, he demonstrated, once again, his creativity. One morning, Villa began gathering his troops at the train station in a way that attracted the interest of curious Magonistas, both officers and troops. In a swift maneuver, fully armed Villistas surrounded the Magonistas, disarmed them, and placed them under arrest without killing anyone.[6] This maneuver was a double victory for Madero. With the Magonistas under control Orozco lost his bargaining power.

The capture of the Magonistas not only secured Madero's power in Chihuahua but also solidified Villa's reputation as Madero's loyal supporter. From then on, Madero kept Villa close to him. He considered Villa a good counterbalance to Orozco and his political ambitions. In other words, Villa had become a key element in Madero's revolutionary strategy. Thanks to Villa's intervention, Madero could now safely lead the revolution in Chihuahua.

THE FIRST BATTLE OF CIUDAD JUAREZ (1911)

After Villa helped Madero reassert his authority among the revolutionary forces of Chihuahua, Madero was ready to attack Ciudad Juarez. On April 7, 1911, Madero, for the first time in control of a substantial and well-organized army, initiated his march to Ciudad Juarez. This army advanced in two frontal columns both consisting of 500 riders, one led by Orozco and the other by Villa. Madero was right behind them with 1,500 support troops.

The advance of Madero's army resembled more a victory march than the march of an army about to engage in a very serious undertaking. People greeted Villa's soldiers and cheered them and federal military garrisons surrendered at their approach. In particular, the towns of Temosachic and Casas Grandes—the place where Madero had suffered his first defeat just a few weeks before—surrendered to Madero because they had only a handful of soldiers and the overwhelmed federal army could not spare additional troops to reinforce them. This image of invincibility inspired more people to join this seemingly triumphant army.

The garrison at Ciudad Juarez had only 700 men to defend the city. That was not enough to repel the revolutionaries, but the soldiers in the garrison hoped that a prolonged siege could give them enough time for reinforcements to arrive and save the city. Indeed, this time it was the revolutionary army that was the stronger and better organized while the federal defenses could only hope to hold their ground. This time the revolutionaries were not planning sneak attacks. The stage was set for the first formal battle of the revolution between two standing armies.

Politics Behind the Siege of Ciudad Juarez

Villa and Orozco were ready to storm Ciudad Juarez when political priorities gave way to military advantages. Porfirio Diaz realized that the widespread nature of the revolution had made him vulnerable and feared that if Ciudad Juarez fell, his reputation of invincibility and his presidency fell with it. In addition, many advisers, particularly Finance Minister Jose Ives Limantour, recommended negotiating with Madero rather than escalating the rebellion. Limantour believed that since Madero was a member of the Mexican elite he could be convinced to compromise, thus avoiding a serious armed conflict and saving Porfirio Diaz's government. Minister Limantour made a convincing argument explaining to Porfirio Diaz that a prolonged conflict could destroy Mexico's strong financial system and scare foreign investors. Limantour's advice suggests that, to some degree, he agreed with the Magonistas' idea that Madero was not a real revolutionary. After all, Madero's main goal was not a comprehensive transformation of the social, political, and economic structures of the country, but rather the establishment of a legitimate democratic regime.

In effect, Madero showed a preference to sit at the negotiating table with representatives of the dictator and avoid the escalation of violence at Ciudad Juarez. Villa and Orozco were taken aback. They were convinced that a revolutionary victory was within their grasp. Porfirio Diaz proposed to Madero that if the revolutionaries were willing to dispose of their weapons he would ban re-elections, distribute land to Mexicans peasants, and increase local autonomy by removing his personally appointed political leaders. Such political concessions seemed reasonable to Madero, but not to his generals. Porfirio Diaz remaining in power, they believed, was a recipe for disaster. Once the revolutionaries disposed of their weapons there was nothing forcing Porfirio Diaz to fulfill his promises.

Orozco and Villa demanded that Madero not accept any peace agreement that did not include the immediate resignation of Porfirio Diaz. Madero's dependency on his generals forced him to decline Porfirio Diaz's offer.

Still, Madero was not convinced that a military victory was the best option to accomplish the aims of the revolution. He was concerned that possible bloodshed in Ciudad Juarez could undermine his prospects as future president of Mexico. Certainly a big portion of the civilian population and the entire federal army would blame him for the resulting death and destruction.

The problem was that Madero was already thinking of how to unite the country as president before even achieving military victory. Madero was contemplating how to defeat Porfirio Diaz without alienating the federal army. As far as he was concerned, the revolutionary forces were only useful for deposing Porfirio Diaz. He had no intention of using them to replace the federal army. His enemy, he felt, was the dictator, not the federal institutions he would need to govern the country.

Madero did not take into consideration the fact that the revolutionary generals expected a reward for their sacrifices. Many of them expected to replace the current army officers and others were politically more ambitious and expected an elected or appointed office. This was a contradiction in the revolutionary leadership. Madero tried to gain the trust of the federal army while his generals sought its total destruction. This impasse threatened the possibility of an assault on Ciudad Juarez.

The Attack on Ciudad Juarez

After a full month of political games, Generals Orozco, Villa, and Luis Blanco (the third most important military leader in Chihuahua) decided to stop talking and take action. They planned to start a confrontation with the garrison at Ciudad Juarez, but they wanted to give the impression that it was an spontaneous and uncontrolled shootout that had escalated into a full-blown battle—a likely incident between two standing armies nervously waiting for their leaders to signal the beginning of hostilities. To hide the fact that this was an organized incident, the three generals left instructions with their subordinates and crossed the border to El Paso. In addition, if his three main generals were away,

Madero could not count on them to intervene fast enough to keep the conflict from escalating.

As expected, random shots at the garrison by the revolutionaries caused a response in kind by the garrison that rapidly began to escalate. A shocked Madero contacted General Juan Navarro, the head of Ciudad Juarez's garrison, and asked him to stop shooting. The overwhelmed general, with limited supplies and a smaller army, told Madero that he was simply trying to defend his position from revolutionary hostilities and that he would stop shooting if the revolutionaries agreed to do the same. Madero was confused. He did not know why his soldiers were attacking without his authorization. He tried to contact his generals but it took him several hours to find them. Finally, an unhurried Orozco came back across the border and met with Madero. The latter immediately ordered Orozco to bring his troops under control. Orozco responded that the attack was well under way and they were overwhelming the federal defenses. He suggested that at this point it was better to finish the job. Madero understood that the damage had been done. He had no option but to agree with Orozco.

The plan to force Madero's hand worked. The victory at Ciudad Juarez was perhaps Madero's easiest and most significant battle of the entire revolution. It demonstrated the massive strength that the revolution had gathered against a declining and unmotivated federal army. The revolutionaries were inspired, more numerous, and better supplied. They even had the luxury of establishing a relay system by which fresh troops constantly replaced exhausted ones at the front. The overwhelmed General Navarro surrendered on the afternoon of the second day. The revolution had won its first significant battle and, as it turned out, a decisive one. The day was May 10, 1911.

The Aftermath of the First Battle of Ciudad Juarez

Opposing opinions arose within Porfirio Diaz's administration when assessing the seriousness of the fall of Ciudad Juarez. His minister of war, General Victoriano Huerta, was not yet willing to concede defeat and told Porfirio Diaz he was confident he could retake the city by mobilizing troops from the south. Minister Limantour disagreed. He was afraid that such a maneuver could expose Mexico City to the southern revolutionaries led by Emiliano Zapata, a highly popular leader of a peasant rebellion south of Mexico City. Limantour was also concerned that Madero's movement was reaching civil war proportions. A protracted conflict, he insisted, would endanger Mexico's fragile economy and increase the anxieties of foreign investors. Porfirio Diaz agreed with his finance minister and understood that he had no other alternative but to accept Madero's conditions.

Thanks to Orozco's, Villa's, and Blanco's unruly behavior, Madero found himself in a stronger position to negotiate the end of hostilities with Porfirio Diaz. He demanded the resignation of the dictator and his vice president, Ramon Corral. On May 21, Porfirio Diaz agreed to the demands and signed the Treaty of Ciudad Juarez. In it he promised to leave the country if Madero promised to leave the federal army intact and disband the revolutionary army. Porfirio Diaz believed that this was the only way to keep the country from falling into anarchy and to guarantee peace and stability in Mexico. Madero agreed with the dictator. Unbeknown to his generals, Madero accepted Porfirio Diaz's terms. On May 26, Porfirio Diaz left for the port of Veracruz in the Gulf of Mexico, boarded the ship *Ypiranga*, and began his permanent exile in Paris; he died in 1915 at age 85.

POLITICS AFTER THE REVOLUTIONARY VICTORY

Madero's attempts to pacify the nation as soon as possible backfired. His attempts caused the anger of both the federal army and his own generals. In order to gain the trust and confidence of the federal army, Madero contacted General Navarro to guarantee his personal safety and that of his soldiers. Madero was planning to use this as a demonstration of his good will toward the federal army. He tried to make clear that his enemy was not the army but the dictator. However, federal officers paid less attention to Madero's gesture than to the humiliation that this defeat brought to their institution. Most officers never forgot that it was Madero who orchestrated their defeat at Ciudad Juarez.

In addition, Madero's friendly gesture toward General Navarro outraged Orozco and Villa. They had hoped to punish General Navarro for a previous incident. On January 2, 1911, this general had executed all the revolutionaries captured in a smaller confrontation at Cerro

Prieto, Chihuahua. They expected Madero to agree that General Navarro deserved the same treatment. Madero refused. Orozco and Villa became outraged and threatened Madero with rebellion. They confronted Madero by gathering all their troops in front of Madero's headquarters—Villa's only direct action against Madero. Once again, Madero showed enormous courage by not paying attention to this obvious act of defiance against his authority. With no demonstration of fear, he stood in front of the troops and addressed them, talking about the promises of a victorious revolution. Madero won the hearts of the soldiers. Orozco and Villa had no alternative but to comply with Madero. Villa learned to respect and admire Madero's courage. However, it had become evident that Madero's revolutionary aims were very different from those of his generals.

Madero's "Revolutionary" Presidency

After the fall of Porfirio Diaz, events did not develop the way Orozco and Villa had expected. Instead of a substantial revolutionary takeover of all government institutions, several members of Porfirio Diaz's government remained in power.

Francisco Leon de la Barra, a member of Porfirio Diaz's cabinet, was chosen as interim president and charged with organizing a new presidential election. Madero was not interested in becoming president in the aftermath of Porfirio Diaz's military defeat. His goal was democracy, and he could claim democratic legitimacy only by being elected president. Nevertheless, his determination to eventually be elected president forced him to give enormous concessions to the existing political elite to the detriment of a truly revolutionary victory. Madero was at the height of his popularity and could expect an easy election, but he refused to use this political capital to incorporate the hopes and aspirations of most of his revolutionary supporters. His political team rapidly became conservative. As far as he was concerned, the revolution's goal was to destroy the dictatorship and install a democratic government. The revolution, according to him, had reached a happy conclusion.

As expected, Madero was elected president of Mexico on October 1, 1911. He received an astonishing 98 percent of the vote, but these numbers represented more the citizens' hope for peace than overwhelming support for the new president's policies. In fact, even before he took office, Madero's political coalition showed multiple fissures that suggested major problems ahead.

The Revolutionary Leadership Mistrusts Madero

An increasing number of revolutionary leaders were appalled that Madero refused to replace the military officers and many key politicians with revolutionary leaders. Many revolutionaries, including Emilio and Francisco Gonzalez, important Maderistas in northern Mexico, joined the revolution with the hope of establishing a new progressive government committed to radical legislation empowering peasants and workers and eliminating the oppressive practices that caused the revolution in the first place. They were frustrated with Madero's apparent belief that all problems would be solved simply because the dictator was gone.

Other more ambitious leaders were disappointed with Madero's lack of gratitude. Most noticeably, Pascual Orozco broke away from Madero when the president refused to appoint him governor of Chihuahua, a post he believed he deserved because of his key role in Madero's victory.

Even more dangerously, some revolutionary leaders refused to respond to Madero's call to end all hostilities and surrender their weapons to the federal army. Most notably, Emiliano Zapata, the most important revolutionary leader of the south, swore to continue fighting regardless of who was president of Mexico. He was not so much interested in the overthrow of Porfirio Diaz. His main goal was to take back the lands that hacendados had taken from the peasants of Morelos. He was determined to continue fighting until that goal was fulfilled.

To the dismay of most revolutionaries, in response to Zapata's refusal to disarm his men, Madero saw no alternative but to send the federal army against him. The president charged General Juvencio Robles with the task of pacifying the state of Morelos. Madero could not have made a worse choice. Robles was a member of the federal army and soon demonstrated the extension of his contempt for the revolutionaries. During his campaign in Morelos he became notorious for his brutality. He staged summary executions of prisoners, burned villages, and coordinated terrorizing campaigns against all peasants in the region, regardless of whether or not they were Zapatistas. Not surprisingly, General

Robles became another liability to Madero's military credentials. In addition, his tactics caused many peaceful peasants to join the Zapatistas for protection, further complicating the situation in Morelos.

Madero did not approve of Robles's brutal treatment of the Zapatistas and decided to replace him with the far more benign General Felipe Angeles. Although a member of the federal army, General Angeles spent most of the revolutionary period studying military tactics in Europe and had never actively fought the revolutionaries. In addition, he agreed with the need for social justice in Mexico and thus was sympathetic to the revolution (he eventually became one of Villa's most influential generals). General Angeles preferred to negotiate with the Zapatistas rather than terrorize them. His campaign achieved considerable pacification of the state of Morelos and gained the respect of Zapata. However, even though Angeles proved an excellent choice for dealing with the Zapatista problem, the damage had been done. Zapata never trusted Madero again.

Madero understood the frustration of his revolutionary generals, but he did not trust their ability to function as part of his government. He did include a select group of educated revolutionaries from the upper and middle classes, but tried to keep most of the rest out of his government. He considered them too aggressive and poorly educated to assume major political responsibilities. As a consequence, the "new revolutionary" government included a considerable number of former Porfiristas who had sided with Madero before the fall of Porfirio Diaz. Soon, many revolutionaries who had been with Madero from the beginning became deeply disappointed.

Villa was one of the few revolutionaries who did not show any political ambitions and refused to turn against the president or question his policies. He believed that Madero was a committed revolutionary and that many people were overreacting, and he publicly acknowledged his commitment to support Madero.

President Madero's Difficulties with the
Conservative Establishment

Madero's efforts to please the officers of the federal army did not produce the results he expected. As promised to Porfirio Diaz, he kept the federal army intact. In addition, he kept most generals in their previous positions and ranks. He even left General Victoriano Huerta in his post as minister of war. However, Madero's gesture was not enough to gain the loyalty of this proud institution. Most officers had a profound respect and admiration for Porfirio Diaz and resented Madero's revolution. In addition, they could never forget that Madero exiled their beloved president and defeated them in war.

Similarly, Madero's conciliatory policies did little to gain the trust and loyalty of the upper classes, particularly because they had benefited so much from the old dictatorship. He, after all, was responsible for the collapse of the government that protected their privileges and wealth. They considered Madero an impostor at the head of a mob that, they feared, he was incapable of controlling. Once again, Madero's policies of reconciliation only furthered his isolation.

The upper classes were terrified of the significance of Madero's victory, and their concern was valid. They were well aware that the revolution had empowered the lower classes and diminished their capacity to control them. Mexico had changed too quickly. The old practices of intimidation to subordinate the lower classes suddenly did not work. Acts of repression or unfair labor policies might now be met with hostile resistance by the lower classes. Hacendados and factory owners understood that they could not count on the protection of the government the way they once did. Unlike Porfirio Diaz, Madero was unwilling to or incapable of sending troops to repress his own supporters in order to protect the interests of the upper classes. This was further evidence, according to members of the elite, that Madero could not prevent anarchy and chaos from spreading throughout Mexico.

President Madero's Political Dilemma

Madero tried to accomplish the impossible: to install a revolutionary government without disrupting the social, economic, and military structures of the old regime. He believed that the economic health of the nation depended on the continuation of the successful policies established by Porfirio Diaz. He had no interest in destroying that successful economic model. In addition, Porfirio Diaz's pro-business policies had benefited Madero's own family. He could not deny the fact that he was a

member of the Mexican elite, which made it very difficult for him to implement radical revolutionary policies. The distribution of land to peasants and a pro-workers' labor code were at the heart of the revolutionary
agenda, but as a wealthy landowner he resisted their implementation.
Madero was at pains to find a middle ground that could guarantee major
social reforms without destroying a successful economic model.

Madero believed that democracy was the solution to his dilemma.
He believed that it could properly guide the upper class as well as the
growing educated middle class, promoting the modernization and economic expansion of the country while providing political reforms such
as guaranteed elections of local representatives, which would allow the
working and middle classes to defend and promote their own interests.
Unfortunately, Madero's middle-ground policy did not please anyone.
The upper classes refused to relinquish their dominant position in society, while the lower classes believed that they deserved real political
power in the federal government after they had contributed so much to
the revolutionary military victory.

Villa Remains Behind the President

Regardless of the gathering evidence that President Madero was slow or
uninterested in fulfilling the promises of the revolution, Villa remained
one of Madero's most loyal supporters. He had been impressed with
Madero's courage and willingness to fight alongside his fellow revolutionaries. He continued believing that the president was committed to
his plan of creating a Mexico based not only on democratic values, but
also on social justice. He never stopped considering Madero an honest
and committed revolutionary.

Villa's trust in Madero was facilitated by the fact that Villa had no
real political ambitions. He considered his job done and believed that
it was time for the better educated members of the revolution to decide
what was best for the country. Villa's most immediate goal had been
fulfilled: the dictator was gone and the Terrazas-Creel clan had been
removed from Chihuahua's government. Villa could now be his own
man and make an honest living without being forced into banditry by
the clan. He was looking forward to retiring from the revolution and
re-opening his butcher-shop business.

However, Villa was not naïve. He understood the new political cli-
mate in Mexico and was worried about the living situation of those
who fought with him. Most of his soldiers had risked too much to surrender their weapons as Madero had suggested, particularly after so
many had lost family members or suffered injuries, complicating their
families' capacity to make ends meet. Villa warned Madero that his un-
willingness to respond to the needs of his supporters and his failure to
disassemble the political and military structures of the old regime was a
terrible mistake that could cost him his life.[7]

Perhaps one of the most important reasons behind Villa's commitment to support Madero was his own personal values. Villa respected
very few things in life more than loyalty. He expected eternal loyalty
from his subordinates and likewise he promised eternal loyalty to his
superiors. In his view, betrayal was one of the worst sins any man could
commit. He rarely hesitated in executing his own men accused of
treason or cowardice. Villa valued his loyalty to Madero over his own
life. However, Madero failed to appreciate this unquestionable loyalty,
one more in a series of mistakes that contributed to Madero's eventual
downfall.

CHIHUAHUA AFTER PORFIRIO DIAZ

Unlike Zapata, who continued fighting the federal government because his peasants still had no lands, Villa trusted Madero because
the situation in Chihuahua had truly changed. Madero removed the
Terrazas-Creel clan from power, which had been one of the main goals
of most Chihuahuans who joined the revolution. In addition, he appointed Abraham Gonzalez governor of Chihuahua. Gonzalez was one
of the most committed revolutionaries of Madero's inner circle and the
person who convinced Villa to join the revolution. Governor Gonzalez
became one of the most progressive governors under Madero's presidency. He had shown honesty, courage, and dedication to social justice during the campaigns against Porfirio Diaz. As governor he moved
quickly to enact changes, particularly in redistribution of land and promotion of local autonomy. Villa had no doubt that the revolution in
Chihuahua was in good hands.

Villa's Sense of Social Justice and Loyalty Toward His Soldiers

Villa had always made clear his loyalty to Madero, but never hesitated to remind him that those who fought to put him in power had the right to expect the support and protection of the government. In this regard, Villa maintained a continuous correspondence with Madero. One of the most common subjects was the responsibility of the government to provide pensions to revolutionary veterans or their widows. Villa never forgot those who fought for him even after he began busying himself in his private businesses and as a husband (he married Luz Corral soon after the end of this first stage of the revolution). Madero, for his part, found it difficult to address Villa's demands, sometimes because of his efforts not to alienate conservative groups, but also because of a lack of money. Villa became increasingly frustrated. He decided to assume full responsibility for ensuring that the needs of his soldiers and their families were met.

Pancho Villa walking away from the execution wall at Torreon after receiving a last-minute reprieve from President Madero, June 4, 1912. (Clendenen Papers, Hoover Institution.)

After Madero failed to respond to the soldiers' needs, Villa began writing angrier letters to the president. In one instance, Villa went as far as ordering the president to "do everything you can in accordance with your responsibilities to see that justice is carried out."[8] When Madero still failed to respond, Villa decided not to wait any longer and took matters into his own hands. He implemented a tactic used by most revolutionaries to provide for their troops while fighting Porfirio Diaz. He selectively raided haciendas belonging to well-known enemies of the revolution, particularly those of the Terrazas-Creel clan. He took their cattle and other resources and used the profits to satisfy the needs of his former soldiers or their widows. It is through actions such as this that the legend of Villa as the "Robin Hood" of the revolution became increasingly popular. More important for the future of the revolution, Villa was distinguishing himself from other revolutionary leaders by the level of commitment he demonstrated toward his soldiers. This trait facilitated Villa's capacity to assemble an army in a relatively short period of time, which was of considerable importance for Villa's successes and his ability to emerge from the ashes of defeat during later stages of the revolution.

The Return of the Terrazas-Creel Clan

President Madero did not approve of Villa's methods of supporting his troops. Raiding haciendas was acceptable during times of war but not in peacetime. He was concerned that Villa was antagonizing Chihuahua's oligarchs. However, he understood the importance of securing the loyalty of people like Villa, particularly at a time when various revolutionary groups across the nation were increasingly disappointed with his regime. More and more revolutionaries were following Zapata's example and taking matters into their own hands. For this reason, instead of confronting Villa, Madero tried to use Governor Gonzalez to keep Villa under control.

However, Governor Gonzalez's revolutionary commitment was more in line with Villa's interests than with those of the president. Not only did the governor refuse to stop Villa from providing for his troops, but he also took decisive steps to destroy the monopoly of power held by the Terrazas-Creel clan in Chihuahua. Villa found in Governor Gonzalez an important ally.

Villa was not aware that Madero was blocking Governor Gonzalez's effort to destroy the power of oligarchs in Chihuahua. Madero, in another effort to smooth his relationship with the upper classes, ordered the governor to stop antagonizing Luis Terrazas and his son-in-law, Enrique Creel. In addition, in the Treaty of Ciudad Juarez, Porfirio Diaz had agreed to leave office together with all the governors, but state and federal legislatures remained in place. This became an impossible situation for Abraham Gonzalez. The congress in Chihuahua consisted mainly of Luis Terrazas's appointees and had no interest in working with the new governor.

Under this difficult situation, Governor Gonzalez tried his best to enact the revolutionary policies that Villa supported. For example, he tried to tax land ownership incrementally in order to make it virtually impossible for the oligarchs to sustain their enormous extensions of land. He also initiated a number of investigations into the Terrazas-Creel clan. Particularly, he investigated fraud allegations regarding Banco Minero, a bank owned by Luis Terrazas. This case became a scandal in Chihuahua. The anti-Terrazas people were outraged at the allegations of corruption and racketeering while those supporting Luis Terrazas were outraged at what they considered a witch hunt against one of the most distinguished families of the state.

Villa was unaware that Madero was in fact strengthening Chihuahua's elite. Madero complicated this situation even more when he asked Governor Gonzalez to join his cabinet in Mexico City. Villa was losing an important ally in the state. The governor was committed to his policies in Chihuahua so he first declined. He was well aware that his departure facilitated the Terrazas-Creel clan regaining the control of the state. Gonzalez had been able to bypass the congress with enormous difficulties and only because of his enormous popularity. He knew that whoever took his place as governor would find it impossible to resist the power of the oligarchs. Madero did not listen to Gonzalez's reasons to stay in Chihuahua and practically forced him to move to Mexico City. Madero's maneuver turned out to be another terrible mistake for his future as president. As oftentimes happened, his policy alienated his revolutionary allies while strengthening the conservative elite that hated him. Now, even in the highly revolutionary state of Chihuahua, the tide was turning against Madero.

THE OROZCO REBELLION

Madero had managed to destroy practically all the support that he had enjoyed in Chihuahua. A state that had been considered solidly on the side of the revolution now became a major concern for his government. A disappointed Orozco was willing to side with the enemy in order to achieve his political ambitions. He created one of the major crises of Madero's government. It is quite possible that without the intervention of Villa, Madero's regime would have collapsed. Thus, Villa's participation against Orozco's rebellion confirmed his position as the most important revolutionary leader in Chihuahua still loyal to Madero.

The Terrazas-Orozco Alliance

Luis Terrazas benefited from Madero's transferring Abraham Gonzalez to Mexico City. Now he was free of any major obstacle and could once again consolidate his power in the state. He also showed increased interest in using this power to destroy Madero's government and perhaps even control the entire country. He understood very well that Mexico after Porfirio Diaz was a different place. He could not depend on the traditional alliance with hacendados and access to their militias that had been the previous source of his power. Now, hacendado-led militias were not as reliable since their workers had the option of deserting to join a revolutionary leader.

Also, Luis Terrazas knew that Pascual Orozco was angry at both Madero and Gonzalez because they had denied him the governorship of Chihuahua. Terrazas approached Orozco and offered him money and resources to initiate a movement against Madero and Gonzalez and the promise of the state's governorship. Orozco agreed, but he did not need to initiate the rebellion. The opportunity to lead a rebellion arrived sooner than he had expected.

The Causes of the Rebellion

Before Orozco could organize his men, Emilio Vazquez Gomez, a lesser leader of the revolution in Chihuahua, lost all hope in President Madero and rose against him. The straw that broke the camel's back was Madero's decision to remove Governor Gonzalez. Before this,

Vazquez Gomez had been infuriated when Madero decided to replace his original running mate for the presidency, his brother Francisco Vazquez Gomez, an important revolutionary leader of Chihuahua, with Jose Maria Pino Suarez, a lawyer from the distant state of Yucatan. The revolutionaries of Chihuahua felt that Madero was weakening their position and actively supporting the oligarchs. Emilio successfully incited a number of leaders to turn against Madero. To everybody's surprise, he was able to take the garrison of Ciudad Juarez—the symbol of Madero's victory.

Pascual Orozco immediately tried to take advantage of this situation and announced his intention to join the revolt. In order not to alienate his fellow revolutionaries, Orozco kept secret his alliance with Terrazas. Emilio Vazquez Gomez recognized Orozco's larger prestige and decided to step aside. Orozco assumed leadership of the rebellion, declaring that the goal of this movement was to guarantee workers' rights and land distribution—two of the main promises ignored by President Madero. The anarchist group led by the Flores Magon brothers and the Zapatistas in the south soon joined Orozco.

Concerned with the situation in Chihuahua, Gonzalez resigned his cabinet position in Mexico City and resumed his job as governor. He tried to use his popularity to appease the rebels, but it was too late. The rebels were now determined to overthrow Madero. Only a handful of revolutionaries in the state remained loyal to Madero. Villa, the most powerful of them, was unsure about his participation in this struggle. What troubled him was the fact that he had to fight his fellow revolutionaries by siding with the federal army. At the beginning he decided to stand on the sidelines and let the federal army defend the president.

Orozco's rebellion spread rapidly and soon became a very serious threat to Madero's presidency. The anger caused by Madero's policies and Orozco's popularity were at the core of this initial success. Orozco demonstrated once again that he was the most skillful military leader of the revolution and achieved quick victories against the federal army. As the rebellion gathered momentum, many more joined Orozco out of sheer opportunism. Very soon, he controlled most of the state. Luis Terrazas secretively continued sponsoring Orozco's rebellion and began to believe that by manipulating Orozco he could destroy not only Governor Gonzalez in Chihuahua, but also President Madero. Terrazas was not alone. In the spring of 1912 most people believed that Madero's fall was only a matter of time.

Villa Saves Madero (Again)

Eventually, Villa realized that Orozco was more interested in increasing his own power and wealth than in remaining faithful to the revolution. He became convinced that Orozco was secretively working for Luis Terrazas when he noticed that Orozco's troops never looted the haciendas belonging to the Terrazas-Creel clan or those of its allies. Villa spoke publicly about this, but he could not offer any real evidence of this secret association. People, however, remained with Orozco for different reasons. Some did not believe Villa's accusations while others, believing that Orozco was the victor, disregarded Villa's accusations and remained with the most likely victor.

Villa knew Orozco's ambitions too well to need further evidence. He finally decided to fight for President Madero. He was convinced that an Orozco victory meant a return to power for the Terrazas-Creel clan. In addition, Orozco's associates, the Magonistas, had had hostile relations with Villa ever since he forced them to submit to Madero's authority.

Villa's Difficulties in Creating a New Army

In the midst of a very successful Orozco campaign, Villa found it very difficult to convince potential soldiers that Madero offered the best guarantees to their interests. Orozco's victories brought back memories of those unexpected revolutionary attacks that overwhelmed Porfirio Diaz's army. One of the most spectacular of these victories took place in the village of Rellano. There, one of Orozco's officers, Emilio Campa, loaded a train with dynamite and let it roll against an oncoming train loaded with federal troops. The carnage and hysteria demoralized the army and further increased support for Orozco.

As more people in Chihuahua sided with Orozco, Villa managed to gather only a few dozen volunteers from western Chihuahua. The villagers from that area knew Villa well and had no real connection with Orozco. However, what Villa did not gain in quantity he gained in quality. These volunteers had fought with Villa before. They were well-seasoned soldiers with excellent fighting skills. Many of them had played an important role in the famous victory of Ciudad Juarez.

Villa Confronts Orozco at Parral

Villa saw an opportunity to attack when Orozco suffered an unexpected setback. The president of the United States, William H. Taft, placed an embargo on selling weapons to the Mexican rebels; thus reducing Orozco's fighting capacity. Orozco sought to compensate for this upset by appropriating the wealth and resources of the city of Torreon in the state of Coahuila, a major commercial hub in northern Mexico. To get there from Chihuahua, Orozco's forces had to traverse the town of Parral. Villa understood the strategic urgency that Torreon represented for Orozco and decided to wait for him at Parral.

The odds for a victory at Parral were against Villa. At this point he could count only 60 men on his side. However, Parral was one of the few remaining towns in Chihuahua still openly loyal to Madero, so Villa also counted on local support. Initially, the people at Parral feared that once Villa settled in the town his soldiers would start looting the town. Once again, Villa knew the importance of public support and made sure that his forces remained well-disciplined. Villa confiscated the resources of wealthy inhabitants to provide for his troops, as instructed and authorized by Governor Gonzalez. The inhabitants were so impressed by Villa's control over his troops that many, including other villagers from nearby towns, soon joined his army.

On April 2, 1912, to the surprise of Madero and federal officers, Villa's meager army managed to resist for several days the attacks of about 1,000 Orozquistas. However, Orozco had an additional 2,500 troops on the way so Villa had no alternative but to flee Parral in the middle of the night. The next morning Orozquista forces entered Parral, looting and destroying property. Orozco's undisciplined and drunken mob presented a clear contrast to Villa's well-disciplined forces. Parral helped clean Villa's violent bandit image. For many now it was Orozco, not Villa, who was perceived as the barbaric leader.

The Significance of Villa's Action at Parral

Villa's resistance at Parral can be considered the beginning of the end of Orozco's rebellion. Regardless of being forced to withdraw, Villa managed to delay Orozco's march toward Torreon by a couple of days. This allowed the federal army enough time to make preparations for the defense of this important city. As a result, Orozco never managed to take it. His hope of gaining access to weapons and wealth there was frustrated and he never recovered. His army was running out of ammunition and supplies, which weighed heavily on the soldiers. In June, he was defeated by federal forces at the Battle of Bachimba, causing many Orozquistas to abandon the cause. Orozco managed to hold his army together until August, but he was incapable of offensive action and withdrew to his stronghold at Ciudad Juarez. His rebellion continued for a few more months, but by now it had ceased to be any threat to Madero's government.

VILLA'S "REWARD" FOR SAVING MADERO

Ironically, Villa's role in destroying a significant threat to Madero's presidency did not bring prize and glory to the now famous revolutionary. Instead, in the aftermath of his resistance at Parral, Villa was humiliated, faced several assassination attempts, and ended up spending eight months in prison.

Villa Faces the Wrath of the Federal Army

Villa had become a victim of his own success. As Orozco's threat declined, the federal army saw in Villa not an ally, but another powerful revolutionary threatening the military supremacy of the federal army. General Victoriano Huerta was not interested in sharing power with revolutionaries and was determined to get rid of Villa. Perhaps the reaction of the federal army was not so surprising, but the reaction of Madero certainly was. As pressure against Villa increased, Madero did little to help the person who saved his presidency.

Initially, Villa had been recognized and honored by Madero for his actions at Parral. He was named "honorary general." He received a uniform appropriate to this rank and medals in recognition of his actions. However, the problem began when Madero, continuing his policy of attracting the support and loyalty of the federal army, ordered Villa and other revolutionaries to place their forces under the direct command of the federal army. This was a big mistake because most officers of the federal army considered the revolutionaries nothing more than brute barbarians. Therefore, they never accepted Villa as one of their own, much less recognized him as a legitimate general.

At the beginning, Villa was not aware of the threat that his honorary promotion represented to his life. In fact, he was excited about joining the ranks of the federal army. He was very interested in learning military strategy and weaponry from his new colleagues. Instead, he only found hostility. Fellow officers made fun of Villa's new uniform, his ignorance in military affairs, and illiteracy.

Villa was not the only victim of the federal army. Huerta and his officers targeted Villa's lieutenants even before Orozco was defeated. Tomas Urbina, for example, was accused of having sacked the Tlahuilo mine, which belonged to an Anglo-American company. Huerta ordered his arrest. Urbina was promptly court-martialed and prepared for execution. In protest, most revolutionaries threatened to abandon the campaign against Orozco, so Huerta decided to spare Urbina's life. However, as the threat from Orozco lessened, Huerta became increasingly determined to demonstrate the superiority of the federal army.

Huerta's Attacks on Villa

As far as General Huerta was concerned, Villa was a bandit who should be either killed or imprisoned. Any excuse would do. He used a dispute regarding a horse between Villa and one of Huerta's officers to begin harassing him. He first accused Villa of having stolen the horse. Angry, Villa told Huerta that he was leaving the federal army and returning to his activities as an independent revolutionary. Under the rules of Madero's revolution, Villa had the right to do so, but under army rules this constituted insubordination. Huerta used this as another excuse to harass him. He accused Villa not only of insubordination but of planning a rebellion against the federal army. On the night of June 3, 1912, he ordered his immediate capture, "dead or alive." The officer in charge of such tasks, Guillermo Rubio Navarrete, went into Villa's camp and found everybody sleeping and no signs of any impending rebellion. He decided to go back to headquarters and report he saw no reason to arrest Villa.

Huerta's Attempts on Villa's Life

Unaware of his perilous situation and of Officer Rubio's overnight expedition, the following morning Villa went to the headquarters to telegraph Madero about his decision to leave Huerta. Huerta used this opportunity to have him arrested and order his immediate execution. Villa was shocked. He broke down and began crying in front of the firing squad. On his knees, Villa pleaded with the officer in charge to spare his life and let him talk to the president to straighten things out. Officer Rubio found Villa against the wall. Aware of the injustice being committed against him, Rubio saved Villa's life for the second time in one day.

Huerta was outraged, but could not act against Officer Rubio because Madero ordered Villa sent to Mexico City. Huerta obeyed but ordered the officer in charge of guarding Villa to use the *ley fuga* (execution from the back in order to claim that the prisoner had attempted to escape). Two attempts against Villa's life were tried during the course of this trip to Mexico City. During the first attempt, General Geronimo Treviño intervened and contravened the order. The second attempt was cancelled because the guard requested a confirmation of the execution from Mexico City.

VILLA'S IMPRISONMENT

Huerta was not someone to give up so easily and tried for the fourth time to kill Villa. As soon as Villa arrived in Mexico City, Huerta had him court-martialed and accused him of treason. Villa received the death sentence yet again, but President Madero changed it to imprisonment. Villa believed that all this was a misunderstanding, but knew that General Huerta was determined to get rid of him. The fact that President Madero intervened gave him hope. He expected that once Madero learned the injustice of his situation, he would be freed.

Madero Refuses to Help Villa

Villa did not expect Madero's reluctance to help him. He had been unjustly accused of theft and treason. None of these accusations were legitimate so Madero had no reason not to intervene. Villa had failed to realize that his imprisonment was politically motivated. Huerta wanted him dead because Villa represented an independent force capable of challenging the military. Madero refused to intervene because he understood that using presidential powers to help Villa would anger not only General Huerta and the federal army, but also many oligarchs and wealthy individuals in Mexico City who saw in Villa the embodiment of the revolutionary chaos and anarchy that threatened Mexico's order and progress. Among those pressuring Madero not to defend Villa was U.S. Ambassador Henry Lane Wilson (no relation to Woodrow Wilson, who became president of the United States in March 1913). Ambassador Wilson sent letters threatening Madero with possible U.S. military intervention if Villa was not punished for his "crimes." Washington had not approved this threat, but Madero was unaware of that fact and took Ambassador Wilson's threat very seriously.

Villa remained in a military prison from June 4 to December 24, 1912. During that period, Villa wrote often to Madero, reminding him that he had always been loyal and that there were no real accusations against him. An ungrateful Madero did not even bother to reply to these letters personally. Instead, he had his secretary write back to Villa informing him that justice would be done, but that President Madero could not interfere with the justice system. Madero's attitude was particularly shocking if one takes into consideration that he had pardoned and freed many federal officers captured during the military phase of the revolution. Indeed, he showed less interest in helping Villa than in helping declared enemies of his government such as Generals Felix Diaz and Bernardo Reyes. These generals, highly popular among Mexico's upper class, were treated by Madero with compassion after both were caught plotting two different coups against Madero. Madero not only intervened to commute their death sentences and place them together in a civilian prison in Mexico City, but he ensured that they also enjoyed substantial contact with the outside world. They took advantage of this opportunity to continue conspiring against the president.

Madero's Presidency Weakens as Villa Remains in Prison

Unfortunately for Madero, the army, the oligarchs, and Ambassador Wilson did not appreciate Madero's attempts to please them by refusing to intercede on Villa's behalf. They considered his position as a sign of weakness and became determined to destroy him. In part because of Madero's victory against Orozco's rebellion, anti-Maderista sentiments were consolidated among conservative groups. The Orozco rebellion allowed the federal army to remove revolutionaries from the state of Chihuahua (including Villa) and take full control of the state. Once Huerta began criticizing Madero, the oligarchs who had supported Orozco moved to support General Huerta. They also hoped that a resentful Villa would turn against Madero and assist in the destruction of the president. Still, Madero refused to see the threat gathering around him and to free Villa, one of the most loyal supporters of his regime.

Villa's Failed Attempt to Escape

By October 1912, after more than four months in prison, Villa was discouraged, but he continued sending letters to the president, always reassuring Madero of his loyalty and alternatively requesting a pardon, a transfer to a civilian prison, or exile, preferably to Spain. Madero continued reassuring him, in letters still written by his secretary, that justice would be done and that Villa needed to be patient. Villa came to believe that Madero was misinformed or misled by reports sent to him by General Huerta and realized that escaping was his only real hope. That month he made his first attempt to escape. However, it was badly planned. He wrongly assumed that some jailers were willing to help him. He realized his mistake in the middle of his escape, but was able to abort the attempt before the jailers realized his intention.

Villa's Successful Escape

Oddly enough, Villa's enemies helped him escape. Some oligarchs and military leaders were interested in breaking Villa's loyalty to Madero so they tried to fuel Villa's frustration with Madero, just as they had done before with Orozco. Using informants in the prison, they filled Villa's head with ideas that Madero had betrayed him and encouraged him to escape and organize a rebellion. They promised him support and provided him with a new set of lawyers who, simultaneously, provided for the first time effective legal counsel and real assistance in helping him escape. Villa did not reject the help, but was cautious about the intentions of all those strangers suddenly willing to help him.

Two months later, on December 24, Villa managed to escape. One of his new lawyers, Carlos Jauregui, was instrumental in the effort. He gave Villa a hacksaw to use to cut the bars of his cell, a suit to disguise him as a lawyer, and a car to drive him away. Villa gladly accepted Jauregui's help but questioned the use of a car. Thinking of a more heroic escape, he suggested a horse. The more practical Jauregui dismissed the idea.

Before his escape, Villa made sure that this action could not be interpreted as an act of rebellion against the president. In early December, during an interview by the *El Pais* newspaper, Villa explained the injustice of his imprisonment. He denounced the lack of evidence against him and restated his unconditional loyalty to the president. In addition, two days before his escape, Villa wrote his last letter from prison to the president. In it, he recognized Madero's merits for having destroyed the dictatorship and attempting to establish democracy. He asked Madero one last time to free him and send him to Spain as proof of his innocence. Once again, Madero refused to help him.

Aware of having no other option, Villa escaped on Christmas Eve, 1912. He left Mexico City in the car provided by Jauregui, made his way to the Pacific coast, then traveled by boat to northern Mexico and finally into the United States. He established his exile residence in El Paso, within view of Ciudad Juarez, the city he had helped conquer to secure Madero's presidency only a year and a half earlier.

Villa in Exile

A month after his escape, tired of waiting for Madero's pardon, Villa wrote his first defiant letter to the president. He indicated that he remained in Texas not because he did not have the means to return to Mexico, but out of respect to the president. He added that if he did not grant him a pardon Madero "had no right to count on [him] in any way."[9] Perhaps this letter was inspired by the oligarchs who were trying to convince both Villa and Madero that they were betraying each other.

Up to this point, Villa had shown total loyalty and admiration for Madero. He fought for him, helped him become president, and saved him from Orozco. Madero, on the other hand, had shown little concern for Villa. Madero simply considered Villa a useful bandit, a mercenary whose abilities were indispensable for the armed phase of the revolution, but not someone for whom it was worth sacrificing political

Villa's artillery massed outside the city under the direction of General Felipe Angeles, prior to the Second Battle of Torreon, March 23, 1914. (Private Collection, Mexico City.)

capital. Indeed, Madero spent most of his presidency trying to gain the respect and support of those who were plotting his destruction: the military, the oligarchs, and the U.S. ambassador in Mexico. Madero's policies, far from attracting their support, emboldened them to take action against him and, this time, Villa was not in Mexico to save him.

THE FALL OF MADERO

Madero's policies of reconciliation with Mexico's military and economic elites not only failed to create the political alliance for which he hoped, but also caused the collapse of his regime in only ten days. This period is known as the Decena Tragica or "Ten Tragic Days." Between February 9 and 18, 1913, the first stage of the Mexican Revolution came to an abrupt end. Following his policy of reconciliation, Madero had refused to execute those found plotting against his regime, especially Generals Bernardo Reyes and Felix Diaz. Their pardon and their ability to coexist in the same prison allowed them to join forces and plot a better-orchestrated coup.

"Ten Tragic Days"

On February 9, 1913, Bernardo Reyes and Felix Diaz launched a joint rebellion against the regime. This was a coordinated military mobilization meant to turn the entire army against Madero. However, some forces remained loyal to him. As a result the rebels failed to reach the presidential offices where they were planning to capture the president. Instead, the bulk of the rebel forces, including Felix Diaz, were forced to seek refuge in Mexico City's arms depot—the Ciudadela. Bernardo Reyes was killed during the initial uprising.

After a few stressful hours, many believed that the uprising had failed. President Madero ordered General Huerta to capture the fortified rebels. However, Madero did not know that General Huerta had been part of this conspiracy from the beginning. The general faked keeping the Ciudadela under siege. Instead of planning an effective strategy to overwhelm the defenders, he used this occasion to satisfy his hatred for the revolutionaries. Huerta selected battalions of revolutionaries that had joined the army to storm the Ciudadela. He kept sending more and more revolutionaries without proper artillery cover, causing heavy casualties and no significant gain. In the meantime the rest of the federal army stood on the sidelines. For several days small arms fire and artillery caused enormous casualties, including many civilians caught in the crossfire, forcing the terrified citizens of the capital to remain behind closed doors.

Huerta also used the siege of the Ciudadela to buy time while trying to secure the support of the U.S. government before moving against Madero. U.S. ambassador Henry Lane Wilson promised that the United States was prepared to recognize a Huerta presidency. Huerta then decided to act. He went to the presidential palace and, taking Madero by surprise, placed him and Vice President Jose Maria Pino Suarez under arrest. He promised to save their lives and send them into exile with their families if Madero resigned the presidency. According to the constitution, upon the president's and vice president's resignations, the secretary of state, in this case Pedro Lascurain, became president of Mexico. However, Huerta convinced Lascurain to resign in his favor as a condition of saving the lives of Madero and Pino Suarez. Even so, Huerta, with Ambassador Wilson's approval, killed Madero and Pino Suarez on February 18.

In El Paso, a horrified Villa learned of the cold-blooded murder of the president. He was incapable of doing anything to stop the collapse of the revolution he had helped create. Huerta was determined to install a new dictatorship similar to that of Porfirio Diaz's. Governors loyal to Madero were forced to declare their loyalty to Huerta or fear imprisonment. Those closer to Madero, like Chihuahua's Governor Abraham Gonzalez, were forced to resign and/or killed. Madero's administration and the revolution were successfully destroyed.

NOTES

1. Friedrich Katz, *The Life and Times of Pancho Villa* (Stanford, CA: Stanford University Press, 1998), 73.

2. Guadalupe Vila and Rosa Helia Villa, eds., *Pancho Villa: Retrato Autobiográfico, 1894–1914* (Mexico: Santillana Ediciones Generales, 2005), 138.

3. Katz, *Life and Times of Pancho Villa*, 77.

4. Paco Ignacio Taibo II, *Pancho Villa: Una biografía narrativa* (Mexico, Editorial Planeta, 2006), 59.

5. Ibid., 61.

6. Katz, *Life and Times of Pancho Villa*, 101.

7. Ibid., 117.

8. Ibid., 150.

9. Ibid., 187.

Chapter 3

AT THE TOP OF IT ALL
(1913–1914)

By the end of February 1913 the revolution appeared dead: President Francisco I. Madero had been killed; Pancho Villa had been humiliated and was living in exile. Pascual Orozco had been defeated, but thanks to the sponsorship of Chihuahua's oligarchs he had joined the federal army; and Emiliano Zapata, the only significant revolutionary still up in arms, was isolated, harassed, and cornered in Morelos. General Victoriano Huerta, the new Mexican dictator, had absolute control of the country. He received considerable support from the armed forces, the Mexican upper class, the Catholic Church, and the U.S. ambassador, all of which Madero desired but never accomplished. Few doubted Huerta's capacity to continue Porfirio Diaz's iron-fisted rule. Most people believed the revolutionaries had lost the goals of the revolution—social justice and democracy—to a new dictator.

THE STRENGTH OF HUERTA'S DICTATORSHIP

In due time, Pancho Villa demonstrated that Huerta's dictatorship actually had feet of clay. Huerta's seemingly solid regime lasted only 17 months, but his fall had an enormous cost in human lives. This second

phase of the revolution became far more violent than Madero's movement. Madero prioritized avoiding the escalation of violence through
negotiations, pardons, and concessions. Similarly, Porfirio Diaz accepted
exile rather than risk a prolonged war. Their attitudes limited the number of dead and the destruction caused by the uprising. However, the
obvious failure of Madero's policies, culminating in his assassination,
taught a powerful lesson to those willing to continue the revolution:
the only way to guarantee success was by aiming at the total destruction of the federal forces. Similarly, Huerta did not approve of Porfirio
Diaz's surrender. The second phase of the revolution saw no negotiated
agreement. Both sides sought total victory over their enemies and most
prisoners faced swift execution.

The revolutionaries had an enormous task ahead of them. They had
to start by re-assembling their armies. Villa was incapable of returning
to Mexico, much less destroying Huerta. The situation looked hopeless
until a relatively obscure leader, Venustiano Carranza, made a courageous stand denouncing the illegitimacy of Huerta's government and
called on all revolutionary leaders to join him against the new dictator.
Eventually, Carranza offered Villa an opportunity to return to Mexico.

Venustiano Carranza Challenges Huerta

Venustiano Carranza's political career began under Porfirio Diaz. Once
a member of Coahuila's political class and a hacendado, Carranza had
been appointed senator of his state by Porfirio Diaz, but decided to
join Madero's movement in 1908 when Porfirio Diaz broke his promise
not to run again for president. Like Madero, Carranza considered democracy the most important goal of the revolution and showed little
interest in addressing social problems. Unlike Madero, however, Carranza understood that a revolutionary government could not rule in alliance with the enemy. He was elected governor when Madero became
president, but refused to follow the president's orders to dismantle the
revolutionary militias from his state and reinstall the federal army. This
decision made Carranza the only governor with enough military independence to denounce Huerta's government.

Carranza was the most powerful elected official to declare war on
Huerta's government. He stated that in order to preserve the consti-

tutionality of the government only those governors elected before the coup could claim legitimacy. He called upon those governors to help him overthrow the dictator. Unfortunately, most governors were either willing or forced to recognize Huerta. A few governors, like Jose Maria Maytorena of Sonora, fled to the United States. Most of those who resisted Huerta and stayed in Mexico suffered imprisonment or execution.

After his bold declaration, Carranza found himself isolated and subsequently forced to flee Coahuila. He sought refuge in the state of Sonora, a more remote state where the federal forces had a weak presence. Despite his precarious situation, he declared himself the First Chief of the Revolution and head of the Constitutionalist Army.

Pancho Villa and other retired or inactive revolutionaries were very interested in responding to Carranza's call. Madero had disappointed many revolutionaries, but Huerta's brutal assassination of the president brought them together against him. In addition, Huerta had begun to replace governors and local authorities with loyalists, including military officers. Many revolutionaries realized that even their limited local autonomy, one of their few tangible achievements under Madero, was in danger. They decided to act, swearing to avenge Madero and joining Carranza's revolution.

Villa Joins the Second Phase of the Revolution

In exile and without an army, Villa was frustrated because he could not find a way to join Carranza's revolution. In the meantime, many revolutionary leaders in Chihuahua attacked the government in very inefficient skirmishes, similar to those that defined the early stages of Madero's revolution. As First Chief, Carranza offered legitimacy to their movement, but had no military expertise to coordinate the uprising. There was an obvious need for a charismatic military leader who could inspire and provide military organization for the rebellion.

Some of Carranza's advisers sought Villa's help and considered ways to bring him back to Mexico. They offered him the means to join them in Sonora, but Villa refused. He was aware that outside of Chihuahua he could not count on popular support and the knowledge of the territory made him a successful revolutionary. Instead, he convinced them to lend him $1,000 so he could plan his return to Chihuahua and create a new revolutionary army. They accepted. Villa crossed the Rio Grande on March 6, 1913. He was at the head of only eight men. His return to Mexico was practically unnoticed, but his charisma and his leadership allowed him to create the largest and most powerful army of the revolution in a relatively short period of time.

THE CREATION OF THE DIVISION OF THE NORTH

Between February and September 1913, revolutionaries fought federal forces without any coordinated strategy, incapable of destroying Huerta's forces or capturing any major cities. During this period, the revolutionary forces presented no real challenge to the new dictator. They were nothing more than a temporary annoyance, and Huerta was confident that he could bring the entire country under control sooner rather than later.

In order to have any real chance at defeating Huerta, the revolution needed to create a well-organized army. Chihuahua, still the major focus of the rebellion, gave the revolutionaries the right place to regroup. Most Chihuahuan revolutionaries fighting Huerta's forces were local leaders interested in defending their own interests. They seldom considered their fight as part of a wider national agenda and were reluctant to surrender their local leadership to an outsider like Carranza. Villa enjoyed the prestige earned during Madero's revolution and many believed that he was the right person to create a united army in Chihuahua. The task was not an easy one. He had to convince all those military leaders to subordinate their power to his command. Villa's charisma was not enough. He was too weak to demand submission. He first needed to demonstrate his own strength and effective leadership.

Villa's Leadership Style

Villa managed to rapidly increase the size of his militia thanks, in part, to his charisma and his reputation for taking good care of his soldiers. In addition, he respected and protected the properties of villagers, while confiscating the property of wealthy hacendados considered enemies of the revolution. He used most of the spoils to support his troops. His appeal was further increased by his tendency to provide justice to those oppressed under Porfirio Diaz's laws. Under his orders, abusive hacienda administrators were humiliated in front of their workers and, in extreme cases, executed. On at least one occasion, he forced a priest to publicly confess to and repent for raping a young girl. Actions such as these created an image of Villa as the people's avenger, inspiring many to join his army.

Soon, Villa headed a respectable militia. In addition, reports that Villa's disciplined forces avoided looting and also protected the properties of U.S. citizens attracted the support of U.S. President Woodrow Wilson, who did not share U.S. Ambassador Henry Lane Wilson's favorable opinion of Huerta. President Wilson considered Huerta a bloodthirsty autocrat who had trampled on the Mexican constitution. U.S. citizens in Chihuahua generally supported Villa so, unofficially, President Wilson allowed arms and money to flow freely across the border into the hands of revolutionaries and, officially, appointed a new ambassador to replace Henry Lane Wilson in July 1913.

Villa Heads the Division of the North

By the summer's end, Villa was rapidly regaining his former reputation as a leader, but he had not yet won any significant battles, which he needed to do in order to convince others of his ability as a military leader. At this point, two other leaders were stronger and more successful than Villa. General Tomas Urbina had taken important cities in Durango. However, Urbina had the reputation of being violent and greedy, unwilling to restrain his troops from looting towns and villages. Many worried that Urbina's violent means would create a negative image for the revolution in Mexico, while losing the support of the United States. Keeping good relations with U.S. authorities was essential to guaranteeing the supply of food, money, and weapons across the border. General Manuel Chao, however, represented a more serious challenge for Villa. A former school teacher, he was intellectually more sophisticated than Villa and enjoyed the political support of the First Chief.

Fortunately for Villa the decision of who would lead the united army was not based on military victories or intellect, but on a *mano-a-mano* between Chao and himself. Chao initially approached Villa and tried to intimidate him by demonstrating his superior intellect, but Villa refused to play Chao's game. Frustrated, Chao moved his right hand toward the handle of his pistol, but his action crossed into Villa's area of expertise. Before Chao was able to touch his own gun, Villa had already pointed his gun at Chao's face. It was now Villa's turn to speak. Chao had no alternative but to listen to Villa's argument and agree with him.[1] In a macho culture in which fighting skills, courage, and bravado were considered important signs of leadership, Villa won the day and election as leader of the united army of the north, which became known as La Division del Norte (the Division of the North). Suddenly, he found himself at the head of 6,000 troops.

Challenges Consolidating the Division of the North

Villa's appointment at the head of the Division of the North did not automatically create a uniformed, disciplined, and united army following a hierarchical line of command. He inherited no formal army, but rather a motley group of fighters, most of whom conditioned their loyalty to Villa according to the instructions of their local leaders. These leaders had joined the revolution for a variety of reasons, did not necessarily consider themselves Villa's subordinates, and reserved their right to disobey his orders. Some joined the revolution to challenge the authority of landowners and bosses. Many others had taken advantage of the chaos and sought personal economic or political gain. Few sought to consolidate a national revolutionary agenda. For many, joining the Division of the North was a means to keep the federal forces from gaining a stronghold in Chihuahua and Durango and to maintain their own local autonomy. Villa's challenge was to transform these leaders with various interests into a united force respecting the chain of command. He had to convince his subordinates that he was indeed the military leader they needed. He sought to achieve this by demonstrating his capacity to capture a major city.

Pancho Villa riding his favorite horse, Siete Leguas, across the Bajada de los Carretones, on the north side of the border town of Ojinaga, shortly after its capture in January 1914. (Private Collection, Mexico City.)

THE CAPTURE OF TORREON

The Division of the North was created to engage the federal army in conventional warfare and obtain significant strategic victories. With this mission in mind, Villa decided to test his new army by capturing the city of Torreon. This city was an important commercial center and a hub of railroad lines connecting central Mexico with the north, including the United States. Its capture would bring important arms and supplies to his army and would allow the use of the railroads to mobilize revolutionary forces.

As Villa prepared his attack on Torreon, his army continued attracting volunteers. As he approached the city his army grew close to 8,000 troops. Increasingly, his problem was how to feed, dress, and arm the growing army, and he believed that a rapid victory in Torreon could provide the supplies he needed. He was also interested in the garrison's artillery. He needed an effective artillery capability in order to protect his advancing armies from the artillery fire from well-defended cities such as Ciudad Chihuahua. In addition to its wealth, the city of

Torreon's geography did not favor defense by artillery so it was an ideal target. Still, the odds were against him: the federal forces were preparing for a long siege and reinforcements were on their way. However, his assault on Torreon benefited from the ineptitude and cowardice of his opponent.

The general in charge of protecting Torreon, Eutiquio Munguia, considered Villa's forces a bunch of bandits with no discipline or military expertise. He underestimated Villa's leadership to the extent that he sent only 500 troops to intercept and destroy the advancing Villistas. Villa had no problem destroying them and proceeded to besiege the city.

Villa Captures Torreon

Villa attacked Torreon on September 29, 1913. In Torreon, Villa used for the first time a strategy that became his fighting trademark, which consisted of continuous day and night massive frontal infantry attacks supported by cavalry charges. The pressure could often overwhelm an enemy. In order to sustain this rhythm, Villa's troops at the front were continuously replaced by fresh troops coming from behind, leaving no time for the defenders to rest and reassess the situation. Night attacks had the additional advantage that while the "insurgents had more or less regular lines of federals to fire at . . . the federals had to fire at the flashes of the insurgents' firearms scattered all over the sides of the hills and in no particular formation."[2] In addition, General Castro, in charge of the defensive artillery firing from Torreon, miscalculated the aim of his guns and the shells fell on his own troops. Overwhelmed, General Munguia panicked and fled the city. His abandoned forces rapidly became disorganized and demoralized and had little option but to surrender the city.

Torreon was Villa's first significant victory of the second phase of the revolution. He was well aware that the eyes of the nation were on him and that the behavior of his troops in Torreon could define his reputation and the population's attitude toward this new phase of the revolution. He ordered his troops to enter the city in an orderly fashion and forbade any form of violence or looting. He was very serious about this order; anyone disobeying was summarily executed. The residents of

Torreon, expecting the worse from the revolutionaries, were impressed by their discipline. However, Villa did not receive the same admiration from his prisoners. The second phase of the revolution was a war of extermination. Villa ordered the execution of all captured army officers. Ordinary soldiers, often forced into military service, were offered the option of joining Villa or joining their officers in front of firing squads. Not surprisingly, soldiers often joined the Division of the North. This practice increased the numbers of revolutionary troops and inspired desertions among federal forces.

The Significance of the Capture of Torreon

The battle at Torreon brought considerable prestige to Villa and important benefits to his army. He supplied his troops with the weapons and resources left behind by the federal army and from confiscations from the city's wealthy merchants. Perhaps more important, Villa now controlled Torreon's rail lines. Trains became an important tool of his military strategy. He used them to mobilize troops and resources, increasing his capacity to fight far from Chihuahua's border. Trains also helped him break the tradition of local fighting that kept most of his forces unwilling to travel far away from their villages. Villa also allowed wives and children to travel along with his soldiers, a decision that not only increased the willingness of his soldiers to become part of a far-reaching army, but it also increased the morale of his troops. Furthermore, women strengthened the Villista forces. In addition to the more traditional roles as cooks and nurses they also became active soldiers. Torreon helped Villa set the foundation for the most formidable army ever created during the Mexican Revolution. Villa had created a well supplied, organized, and disciplined army out of the motley bands that had initially formed the Division of the North.

VILLA'S CONTROL OF CHIHUAHUA

Enjoying his rising strength and prestige as well as a growing optimism among his troops, Villa believed that he was now ready to take control of the state of Chihuahua. He expected to accomplish this by attacking the state's capital. However, General Salvador Mercado, in charge of guarding Ciudad Chihuahua, proved far more competent and brave than Torreon's defender, General Munguia. But Villa was confident. His troops were stronger than ever and for the first time he had the guns and howitzers needed for artillery support, most of them captured at Torreon. However, Villa remained uncertain about the appropriate use of artillery and did not have anyone sufficiently competent to use it properly. Thus, his artillery did not make any significant difference in the short run. Instead, his attempt to capture Ciudad Chihuahua was a fiasco. For three days he charged against the well-disciplined defenders of the city. Exhausted and demoralized by the enormous waste of lives, Villa realized that he was not going to capture Ciudad Chihuahua and retreated.

The Capture of Ciudad Juarez

The prestige that Villa had gained only a few days before at Torreon rapidly crumbled after his retreat from Ciudad Chihuahua. He needed to regain the confidence of his generals with another victory. Villa decided to try his luck again at Ciudad Juarez, the city that he helped capture in 1911, securing Madero's victory. The task was not an easy one. Ciudad Juarez was also well defended and Villa's troops were demoralized. Villa had the additional problem of not being able to use his aggressive frontal attacks without risking having bullets flying into El Paso, causing casualties there and provoking the anger of the U.S. government.

However, once more luck and ingenuity were on Villa's side. As his forces approached the city, he managed to capture a federal train delivering supplies to Ciudad Juarez and then forced the train dispatchers along the way to telegraph the normal progress of the supply train. However, Villa had a different idea about what the train should deliver to Ciudad Juarez. Consequently, he loaded the train with 2,000 troops and sent his version of a Trojan Horse to the heart of the city. The train arrived at two in the morning of November 15, 1913. The defending forces were not expecting Villa so most officers were at the time enjoying the city's bars and bordellos. The federal soldiers were taken by complete surprise and most did not even manage to escape. The city fell into Villa's hands with hardly a shot fired.

Ciudad Juarez and Villa's Negative Reputation

Following the fall of Ciudad Juarez, Villa ordered the execution of all federal army officers, with only one exception. General Francisco Castro's life was spared because he had been involved in saving Villa's life when Huerta had ordered his execution. Although the execution of officers had become a common practice on all sides of the conflict, these executions were particularly harmful to Villa's reputation. His executions were not any different from those committed by other revolutionaries or the federal army. However, while most commanders executed their prisoners at night, Villa executed his prisoners in broad daylight. Villa's intention was to intimidate his enemies and inspire more desertions from the federal forces, but making these executions public gave ammunition to his enemies, who depicted Villa as a bloodthirsty bandit.

This propaganda potentially eroded U.S. support for Villa as well. President Wilson despised Huerta, but was also wary of the possibility of helping enthrone another tyrant. Villa was able to limit the damage because his own propaganda machine pointed out the lack of chaos and looting in the cities under his control. President Wilson decided not to pay too much attention to the anti-Villista propaganda and publicly expressed his support for Villa.[3]

The Defense of Ciudad Juarez

Soon after the fall of Ciudad Juarez, Villa had to defend the city from the federal forces moving north from Ciudad Chihuahua. Villa's troops lacked enough supplies to sustain a long siege so he decided to confront the federal forces on a terrain favorable to his army. He chose Tierra Blanca, a small railroad station outside Ciudad Juarez. The terrain surrounding Tierra Blanca consisted of sand dunes and low hills. By placing his troops on the hills Villa forced the federal army into the lower dunes where the troops were slow and vulnerable and the artillery was likely to get stuck.

The two armies met on November 23, 1913. Villa launched his frontal attacks causing heavy casualties on both sides. The federal army was able to hold its ground for three days. Perhaps afraid of a repeat of his failed attempt at Ciudad Chihuahua, Villa ordered an all-out attack with his cavalry, hitting the flanks of the enemy, which finally broke the federal forces' formation. He added a last blow by sending a locomotive loaded with explosives into a train carrying federal reinforcements. The resulting explosion caused panic and chaos among the already exhausted federal troops, who disbanded, leaving artillery and other resources behind.

Rodolfo Fierro: Villa's Primary Executioner

During the battle at Tierra Blanca, Villa was particularly impressed by the courage demonstrated by one of his soldiers named Rodolfo Fierro. During an attack, Fierro rode his horse to chase a train loaded with enemy troops. He reached the locomotive, jumped in, killed the engine crew, and stopped the train so Villa's forces could destroy the enemy soldiers.

Fierro was courageous, but he was also known as someone who enjoyed killing people. He represented the opposite image of how Villa wanted his army perceived. Yet Villa admired Fierro's courage so much that he decided to incorporate him as part of his elite unit, *Los Dorados* (the Golden Ones). Fierro "would do more to harm [Villa's] reputation than probably any other of his associates."[4] Fierro's cold-blooded killings and his association with Villa were used by Villa's enemies to fuel their anti-Villa propaganda. Fierro was indeed some sort of bloodthirsty monster. On one occasion, he offered over 200 prisoners the option to run for their lives. If they managed to cross a yard and jump over the opposite wall he would spare their lives. The only caveat was that they had to do that in groups of ten while Fierro shot at them. He killed all the runners but one who managed to jump over the wall.[5]

The Capture of Ciudad Chihuahua

Villa's victory had decimated General Munguia's forces, leaving Ciudad Chihuahua exposed. The federal army had left only 200 soldiers to keep order in the city while moving north to fight Villa at Tierra Blanca. Villa's troops simply moved in and occupied the capital of Chihuahua. In the meantime the small group of defenders fled to Torreon, which Villa had abandoned when he moved to Chihuahua. Villa was not only in possession of the two most important cities of the state, but having captured the capital city he found himself the de facto leader of Chihuahua. Villa was rapidly becoming the most successful and powerful leader of the revolution, leading over 10,000 soldiers and governing the largest state of the country.

GOVERNOR VILLA

Villa had not prepared to be the political leader of Chihuahua. He did not join the revolution in order to become a politician. He fought believing that the professional politicians would take over after he accomplished his military goals. Politicians at the state level were often members of highly educated upper and middle classes familiar with law and administration. This time, however, Villa and his generals had been fighting practically without a political leader. Carranza provided constitutional legitimacy to the uprising against Huerta, but they considered him a foreigner in Chihuahua. It all indicated that Villa had to become governor.

Silvestre Terrazas: Villa's Political Right Hand

Villa knew his poor education, lack of political expertise, and lack of administrative skills were serious limitations if he became governor, so he offered the post to Silvestre Terrazas (no relation to the Terrazas-Creel clan), a local journalist who had been writing in support of Villa and had helped him obtain weapons from the United States. Terrazas refused. He felt that as a civilian governor he would be incapable of wielding effective authority over most revolutionaries. Villa then suggested that he could take the governorship and Terrazas could administer the state as his personal assistant. Terrazas agreed. Together, Villa and Terrazas created an effective revolutionary government for the state of Chihuahua.

Villa's Social Policies

Villa governed Chihuahua only from December 8, 1913 to January 7, 1914. During this very short tenure he brought about dramatic changes. As soon as he took office, he announced three decrees: the confiscation of properties of all the enemies of the revolution, particularly Spaniards; the construction of schools to empower the poor; and in the interest of the protection of city dwellers, he ordered his troops to not drink alcohol and he increased policing.

Villa acquired a particular hatred of Spaniards from conversations he had with Zapatistas while in prison. They told him stories describing centuries of Spanish exploitation of Mexicans, beginning with the Spanish conquest of the Aztec empire. In addition, in Chihuahua, Spaniards were often the merchants, landowners, and managers abusing peasants and workers. Villa also accused the Spaniards of celebrating the assassination of Madero and supporting Huerta's government. He declared all Spaniards enemies of the revolution. Villa also expelled Chinese people from the state, but his reasons for doing this were less clear. Apart from the Spanish and Chinese, Villa showed respect to foreigners, particularly U.S. citizens, and their properties.

Perhaps Villa's most important personal goal as governor was the creation of new schools for the eradication of illiteracy. All throughout his life, he regretted not having the opportunity of an education. Even as the leader of one of the most powerful armies in Mexico, he felt vulnerable in front of politicians, intellectuals, lawyers, and army officers due to his lack of education. Villa was convinced that the abuse the poor endured from the wealthy and powerful could be alleviated, in part, with education. In 1914 he ordered the construction of some 100 schools and used one of Luis Terrazas's haciendas, the Quinta Carolina, to establish the Universidad Fronteriza (University of the Border).

Villa's dry law and heavy policing helped him attract the support of an upper class afraid of chaos and anarchy. Thus, Villa managed to unite both the lower and upper classes behind his government. Furthermore, his expulsion of the Terrazas-Creel clan from Chihuahua was also supported across classes. The clan not only had abused peasants and workers for decades, but had restricted job opportunities for professionals and entrepreneurs who did not enjoy connections with the clan.

Villa's new power did the most to change his image from that of a bandit to that of a successful, just, and charismatic revolutionary. His actions complied with the image of a humane leader. After occupying Ciudad Chihuahua, Villa decided not to execute any prisoners. He also forbade extra-judiciary vendettas of people trying to take advantage of the revolutionary upheaval to settle old personal disputes. He enforced this order by using the army to police the city. Chihuahua under Villa enjoyed the most peaceful and stable times of the entire 10-year revolution.

Villa's peace also produced economic stability. Residents of Ciudad Chihuahua had been suffering from economic decline due to all the battles in the area and the destruction of infrastructure, particularly railroads. Showing compassion for the poor and other victims of the civil war, he used confiscated properties from Spaniards and Terrazas-Creel allies to relieve the population, but left the rest to pursue their business under stable conditions.

The Terrazas' Wealth Serving the Revolution

Luis Terrazas's wealth was particularly important for supporting Villa's troops, reducing the need for looting. In addition to cattle, Villa tapped into Terrazas's cash. In one particular case, he was told that Luis Terrazas's son, Luis Jr., was hiding in the British consulate. He had remained in the city unsuccessfully expecting to bribe Villa the same way his father had done with Orozco. However, Villa was not Orozco. In complete disregard for British diplomatic immunity Villa stormed the consulate and captured him. Villa's bodyguards believed that the Terrazas family kept substantial money hidden in the walls of the Minero Bank owned by the family. They forced Luis, Jr. to reveal its location. He refused to talk so they tried to scare him by hanging him, but carefully enough to avoid killing him. Fearing for his life, he confessed that the gold was hidden in the ceiling of the bank, right next to a particular column. Villa's men probed the ceiling and, sure enough, they were showered with gold.[6]

The Limits of Villa's Revolutionary Government

Regardless of his success as governor, Villa found himself sometimes unable to satisfy his supporters' specific demands. For example, he was unable to expand local autonomy to the villagers of his state, one of their most important demands. His political, economic, and military policies depended on a centralized government that allowed him to enact policies according to the general interest of the state and not to the local interest of villagers. The people of Chihuahua acquiesced to the continuation of this political order because they believed that these were extraordinary circumstances and that Villa had their best interest in mind, so they trusted that after the revolution they would get what they were fighting for.

One of Villa's main challenges as revolutionary governor was the issue of land reform. Many expected him to waste no time expropriating lands from the wealthy and giving them to the poor and those affected by Terrazas's abusive law of 1905. He failed to do this, not for lack of interest, but because he faced a difficult dilemma. There was still a lot of fighting to be done and offering land to his soldiers would have caused many to eagerly trade their rifles for a plough. Conversely, it would have been unfair to his soldiers if he distributed the land to peasants and daily laborers who were not fighting with him. Villa managed to ease the situation by promising that the distribution of land would take place after the revolution. He had temporarily weathered the storm, plus he managed to attract more people who found a concrete reason to fight for Villa's vision of a postrevolutionary Mexico.

Villa's Vision of a Postrevolutionary Mexico

As governor, Villa promoted a version of a postrevolutionary Mexico that went beyond everyone's original expectations. He envisioned an entirely new social order. He dreamed of a Mexican republic with workers organized in communes and without a standing army. He knew firsthand that soldiers were forced into the military by selfish tyrants. However, he believed in an army of the people to defend the country against those tyrants and from foreign aggression. In order to fulfill this vision, he proposed to adapt the Chihuahuan model of the military colonies that fought the Apaches. Every young male would receive military training so they could join an army in moments of need. At the same time, military training, he thought, would help workers become a disciplined and efficient labor force. This national project turned out to be a utopia; Villa was never able to implement his vision even at the state level.

Villa Steps Down as Governor

Villa's success as governor worried Venustiano Carranza. He considered Villa's meteoric rise a threat to his own authority and political future. This was the origin of a crack that began to divide the revolutionary leadership even before Huerta was defeated. Carranza tolerated a certain amount of independence from his generals on the battlefield, but he drew a line at the political arena. Carranza pressed Villa to step down and appoint Manuel Chao governor of Chihuahua. Villa agreed to step down. This eased the tension between Villa and Carranza, at least for some time. Carranza believed that he had gained political control of Chihuahua, but this was illusory.

Regardless of his popularity as governor, Villa was not a politician and was happy to comply with Carranza's demand. His interest in governing was limited to implementing specific reforms. As soon as he enacted the most urgent ones he found governing tedious. His real interest was in the Division of the North and fighting Huerta. Carranza's attempt to weaken Villa's political power was not as successful as he had believed. Chao was appointed military governor, which meant that he was Villa's subordinate, and Villa made sure that Silvestre Terrazas remained as adviser to Governor Chao.

The U.S. Government Supports Villa

Villa's policies and actions received wide popular support and strengthened his position as leader of Chihuahua. In January 1914, he was once more publically acknowledged by U.S. President Woodrow Wilson, who recognized him as the man best suited to govern not only Chihuahua but the whole of Mexico.[7] President Wilson believed that Villa had demonstrated limited political ambitions, thus he would be capable of consolidating democracy by not seeking to perpetuate himself in office. Furthermore, Villa shared the culture of the frontiersmen who saw no nationalist problem collaborating with Americans.

The alternative to a possible President Villa was Carranza. Unlike Villa, Carranza was an uncompromising nationalist who could complicate U.S. policy and interests in Mexico. President Wilson understood that Villa's perception of Mexican sovereignty was more flexible and in tune with U.S. interests.

Villa's access to weapons, supplies, and money was further enhanced by his signing a contract with the Mutual Film Corporation. This U.S. company offered Villa $25,000 and 20 percent of revenues from movie screenings of original footage of his military campaigns.[8]

Villismo in Chihuahua without Governor Villa

In 1914, Governor Chao consolidated Villismo in Chihuahua. Although appointed by Carranza, Chao remained a Villista at heart. He shared Villa's revolutionary ideals and continued implementing the political, social, and economic reforms initiated by Villa. He established a welfare state in which some of the vast resources of the wealthiest members of Chihuahua's society were used for subsidies for the poor. He also formalized Villa's economic system. Revenue was generated primarily from selective confiscation of properties, from taxing exports to the United States, and from Villa's own printed money. This new currency was accepted not only in Chihuahua, but also in the United States. As long as the economy of the state was stable and Villa remained the strongman of the revolution, his currency enjoyed a fair value against the dollar.

For Villa, controlling Chihuahua was not so much a matter of political power as a way to sustain his massive army. Villa depended on state revenues. In addition, Chihuahua's shared border with the United States represented a lifeline that provided the resources, weapons, money, and diplomacy that Villa needed to keep his military machine running. With this in mind, Chao continued Villa's pro-U.S. policies and made certain to protect U.S. properties from confiscations, violence, and tax increases. However, many U.S. entrepreneurs, particularly miners, refused to resume work as long as the fighting continued. The result of this pro-U.S. policy meant that primarily Mexican businessmen and landlords carried the load of sustaining Villa's government and army.

THE WEAKNESS OF VILLISMO

During late 1913 and most of 1914, Villa blossomed into the most powerful and charismatic leader of the revolution. Yet, even when he stood at the top of it all, careless economic policies and poor judgment exposed the weaknesses of Villismo and threatened its very survival.

Villa's Economic Vulnerability

Even during the golden years of Villismo in Chihuahua, observers could already see problems in his economic policies, problems that eventually contributed to Villa's sudden downfall in 1915. As the strongman of the state, Villa had access to Chihuahua's enormous wealth, but he failed to develop strategic economic policies guaranteeing long-term economic growth and investment. Instead, he consumed the state's resources while providing for his ever-growing army and social policies. The basis of Chihuahua's economy was cattle, but Villa's massive army and welfare policies were depleting the cattle stock. Therefore, Villa began to depend more and more on printing money to finance his expenses, causing a depreciation of the currency. When merchants began refusing his currency, inflation kicked in, with serious consequences for the poor. He did not understand the dynamics of a market economy so he blamed the merchants and accused them of being greedy and selfish. Because of his lack of economic expertise, Villa failed to take early measures to solve the crisis, and his dependency on U.S. support increased. Villa's economic policy was his Achilles's heel. Success depended on his ability to end the revolution as soon as possible, but his struggle with Carranza prolonged the conflict with catastrophic results.

The Benton Affair

President Wilson's support and the flow of resources that he allowed into Mexico became increasingly important for Villa's finances, but in February 1914 Villa suddenly found himself at risk of losing it. The reason was an incident with a British citizen named William Benton. Benton was a Scotsman who had married a wealthy Mexican woman, acquiring riches and land. A close associate of Luis Terrazas, Benton did not enjoy Villa's sympathy. Making use of the land laws of 1905, Benton expanded his lands to close to 320,000 acres, including communal lands that had been used for centuries by the villagers of Santa Rosa and Santa Maria de Cuevas. Benton fenced his land, cutting the villagers' access to their traditional sources of farmland, water, wood, and grassland for their animals. Villagers took advantage of the revolution and took these lands by force. In addition, Villa's men took Benton's cattle.

On February 15, an outraged Benton appeared in Villa's office demanding the expulsion of the villagers from his land and compensation for the stolen cattle. Villa and Benton had a long and heated quarrel. Even today it is unclear exactly what really happened in that room. At some point during their exchange of insults, Benton made a move; some claimed that he was reaching for a handkerchief while others claimed that he was reaching for his gun. In any event, before he could reach for anything, he was dead. Some believe that Villa shot him; others argue Rodolfo Fierro pulled the trigger. Other reports say that Benton was taken prisoner and later executed. Villa did not think much of this incident. Benton was not a U.S. citizen and he was a well-known supporter of Huerta's regime. Like thousands of other victims of these violent times, he was taken away and unceremoniously buried. The problem for Villa began when Benton's wife, knowing that he was last seen visiting Villa, inquired about her husband. After she received no answer she sought the help of the British consulate in Ciudad Juarez. The British government, which employed a policy of refusing to negotiate with revolutionaries, asked the U.S. consulate to investigate Benton's disappearance. Villa suddenly found himself in the middle of an international scandal.

The Benton affair tarnished Villa's reputation and improved Carranza's. It also helped Villa's enemies highlight his barbaric nature, pointing out that even influential foreigners were in serious danger when Villa was in charge. The British government pressured President Wilson to investigate. Taken aback by U.S. pressure to explain the whereabouts of Mr. Benton, Villa did not know how to react. He first said that Benton was killed because he threatened his life. Confused by the increasing pressure, Villa added that he shot him in self-defense. Finally, he said that Benton tried to kill him so he had him court-martialed and executed by a firing squad. To support this story he exhumed the body and riddled it with bullets.

Fortunately for Villa, Carranza told him that he would take care of the situation. Carranza saw this affair as a political opportunity to act effectively as the First Chief of the revolution and Villa's boss. Carranza instructed Villa not to allow anyone to do an autopsy on the body; forensic doctors could clearly tell if the wounds were inflicted on a dead body. The pressure by the Wilson administration escalated, protests against Villa increased in the newspapers, and several public demonstrations were organized in the United States. President Wilson tried to organize an international commission to investigate, but Carranza condemned such a plan as a violation of Mexican sovereignty and created, instead, a revolutionary commission. Carranza added that the United States had no role in this case because Benton was a British citizen. Thus, the British government could negotiate with Carranza and recognize his authority, or not negotiate with him and forget the issue. The plan worked perfectly: President Wilson was careful not to infringe on Mexican sovereignty and the British ambassador refused to talk to Carranza. The scandal dragged on, but without formal negotiations the crisis passed.

VILLA BEYOND CHIHUAHUA

The Benton affair damaged Villa politically and threatened the flow of resources from the United States, but did not dampen the effectiveness of Villa's army. In fact, during the spring of 1914, Villa overwhelmed Huerta's forces while many other revolutionary forces around the country were having a difficult time confronting them. Villa became indispensable in the effort to defeat Huerta and began fighting beyond Chihuahua.

General Felipe Angeles: Villa's Political and Military Adviser

Villa was admired for his military skill but many, perhaps including Villa himself, doubted the capacity of Villismo to dominate national politics. Villismo needed a man with the intellectual and political capacity to capitalize on Villa's military strength and spread a Villista presence around the country. On March 15, Villa embraced such a man: General Felipe Angeles. Fierro's antithesis, General Angeles contributed perhaps more than any one else to the cause of improving Villa's reputation as a national leader.

Before the revolution, General Angeles had been a career soldier who benefited from Porfirio Diaz's patronage. He attended the Mexican Military Academy and eventually became a professor there, teaching mathematics, ballistics, and artillery. His intellect was recognized among his peers and superiors so Porfirio Diaz sent him abroad to learn the latest in weaponry and military strategy. While he had belonged to the federal army he never fought the revolutionaries because between 1910 and 1911 he was studying in France.

After Madero became president, Angeles returned to Mexico, joined the revolutionary government, directed the military academy, and successfully pacified the Zapatistas. Unlike Madero, Angeles did not trust Huerta. During the Ten Tragic Days, he noticed Huerta's calculated failure to destroy the perpetrators of the coup, his careless use of revolutionary soldiers to storm the Ciudadela, and his negative comments against President Madero. For his part, Huerta was aware of Angeles's loyalty to Madero and considered him a threat to his plan.

In February 1913, Huerta had arrested Angeles together with President Madero and Vice President Pino Suarez. Angeles's life was spared thanks to the timely intervention of U.S. Ambassador Henry Lane Wilson, who did not show the same interest in saving President Madero's life. Angeles escaped to Sonora where he joined Carranza and his revolutionary army. However, most of Carranza's generals questioned Angeles's loyalty while Angeles questioned Carranza's revolutionary commitment. Everybody was relieved when Carranza sent Angeles to join Villa's army.

Villa gladly welcomed among his ranks an officer well educated in intellectual and military matters. Villa could now make good use of the artillery he had collected from fleeing federal forces. As a member of the Division of the North, Angeles proved himself not only an invaluable artilleryman, but also one of Villa's most influential military and political strategists. President Wilson was aware of Villa's limited intellectual expertise and began considering Angeles as a potential Villista president. By now, the Benton affair was practically forgotten so President Wilson re-approached Villa, supporting his branch of the revolution.

The Second Occupation of Torreon

With Angeles by his side, Villa could now transform the Division of the North into a highly effective and professional army capable of destroying Huerta. He decided to retake Torreon and began his march to Mexico City. Along with an effective artillery capability, trains now formed an integral part of Villa's military strategy. Trains moved thousands of men, women, and children increasingly further away from their villages and localities. They traveled mostly on train roofs because the cars were often full of horses, supplies, and artillery pieces. The movements of trains were not telegraphed to avoid interceptions and to take the enemy by surprise. On March 22, 1914, Villa's forces began to besiege Torreon.

The federal forces understood the strategic importance of this city and fortified it heavily. For over a week, they managed to contain Villa's massive charges, but on April 3, Villa broke the defenses and took the city. This was the bloodiest battle of the revolution so far. Villa lost close to 2,000 of his men. The federal forces lost probably twice as many. Following his victory, Villa proceeded to execute the officers captured while a considerable number of federal soldiers joined his army.

Villa's permanent occupation of Torreon meant a wealth of supplies to replenish his army. As always, Villa did not allow looting. Instead, following revolutionary protocol, he confiscated the lands from Huerta's sympathizers or those who abandoned their properties. In addition, all Spanish residents of Torreon were rounded up, sent to the United States, and their properties confiscated. As he had done as governor of Chihuahua, he kept most of the appropriated lands under the administration of the revolution. Some resources were used to sustain his army and the rest to ease the sufferings of city dwellers affected by the conflict.

The battle for Torreon was a turning point in the struggle against Huerta. Villa had become indisputably the most powerful military man in Mexico. Huerta was vulnerable and placed his last hope on the possibility of stopping Villa at Zacatecas. If he failed, Villa would have little difficulty entering Mexico City and capturing him. Unfortunately for Villa, this also worried Carranza. The First Chief was determined to remain the political leader of the revolution, but Villa's victories were now rendering Carranza increasingly irrelevant. Even before Huerta's government collapsed, the revolution was entering a new phase with the revolutionaries increasingly divided into two antagonistic camps. Carranza began a policy of harassment designed to keep Villa from capturing Zacatecas.

The revolution suffered an irreparable division of its leadership. This division did not keep the revolution from defeating Huerta, but eventually produced a civil war, the third and bloodiest phase of the 10-year long revolution.

NOTES

1. Frank McLynn, *Villa and Zapata: A History of the Mexican Revolution* (New York: Carroll and Graf Publishers, 2000), 170.

2. Friedrich Katz, *The Life and Times of Pancho Villa* (Stanford, CA: Stanford University Press, 1998), 307.

3. Paco Ignacio Taibo II, *Pancho Villa* (Mexico: Editorial Planeta, 2006), 226.

4. Katz, *Life and Times of Pancho Villa*, 269.

5. Ibid.

6. Taibo, *Pancho Villa*, 276.

7. Katz, *Life and Times of Pancho Villa*, 311.

8. Robert L. Scheina, *Villa: Soldier of the Mexican Revolution* (Washington, DC: Potomac Books, 2004), 32–33.

Chapter 4

A REVOLUTION DIVIDED AGAINST ITSELF (1914–1915)

Almost from the beginning of the second revolutionary uprising, Pancho Villa did not respect or trust Venustiano Carranza. He questioned Carranza's legitimacy as the Constitutionalist leader of the revolution, and did not recognize Carranza's authority over the territories that Villa had conquered. Carranza feared Villa's rise as a political leader, which was why Carranza pressured Villa to step down so he could appoint General Manuel Chao as governor of Chihuahua.

While Carranza succeeded at forcing Villa out of office, Villa's political influence in the region stayed strong. Ideologically, Chao was close to Villa's political agenda and had little in common with Carranza's more limited revolutionary goals. Indeed, Chao was a Villista at heart and, despite being a Carranza appointee, he showed a better disposition toward Villa. Villa had become a serious threat to Carranza's ambitions. Even if Villa did not aspire to become president of Mexico, his new associate, General Angeles, was considered by many the frontrunner to take the presidency once Villa reached Mexico City. Villa, not Huerta, had become Carranza's most formidable opponent.

THE UNITED STATES FACTOR

The U.S. government's attempt to influence the revolution further complicated the division between Villa and Carranza. An incident between the United States and Mexico exposed the different attitudes that Villa and Carranza had toward the United States. The Wilson administration became aware that Huerta, attempting to break the U.S. arms embargo, was expecting a shipment of weapons from Germany at the port of Veracruz in the Gulf of Mexico. U.S. Marines occupied the port of Veracruz on April 22, 1914.

President Wilson expected the revolutionary leadership to approve this occupation since it caused a negative effect on their enemy. Unaware of Mexican sensitivities toward U.S. involvement in national affairs, he was taken aback when the people of Veracruz, not Huerta's government, resisted the U.S. occupation. Carranza was an uncompromising defender of Mexican sovereignty and immediately condemned President Wilson's actions.

Villa had a more practical approach toward the incident. He was less concerned about nationalist pride and sovereignty issues than with defeating Huerta. He recognized that this occupation weakened Huerta and facilitated defeating him. Furthermore, his army's strength depended on keeping a good relationship with the Americans. Villa not only smuggled arms and supplies from the United States, but his army included many U.S. mercenaries—resembling, at times, the joint Mexico-U.S. efforts against Apache raids. In addition, for Villa's more parochial culture, Veracruz was a distant, almost foreign, territory that had little to do with his homeland. Unlike Carranza's strong nationalism, for Villa the idea of national sovereignty was less significant than defeating Huerta.

The representative of the U.S. government in Ciudad Juarez continued lobbying and buying weapons for Villa. The United States decided to finally put aside the Benton affair and fully support Villa.

CARRANZA DETERMINED TO STOP VILLA

Carranza's political career depended now on his ability to stop Villa's march to Mexico City. Villa was already preparing an attack on Zacatecas, the last of Huerta's major strongholds before Mexico City.

A desperate Carranza ordered Villa to move north and attack the city of Saltillo instead. This command made no military sense. The Division of the Northeast, under General Pablo Gonzalez, was closer and was strong enough to take Saltillo. Villa understood that this was a political decision tailored to keep him from a possible victory at Zacatecas. Villa understood that not obeying Carranza meant an act of rebellion so he decided to respect the line of command and subordinated himself to Carranza's authority.

Adding insult to injury, Carranza named General Panfilo Natera, one of Villa's subordinates, commander of the newly created Army of the Center and charged him with leading the attack on Zacatecas. To secure a victory, Carranza ordered General Alvaro Obregon, the leading general of the army of the Northwest, to support Natera at Zacatecas. Villa had been effectively removed from participating in one of the most strategically important battles against Huerta. He was furious, but remained obedient to Carranza.

VILLA'S INDISPENSABILITY

Villa grudgingly turned his back on Zacatecas and headed for Saltillo. He commanded 10,000 troops and carried 36 pieces of artillery under the command of General Angeles. The federal army garrisoned at Saltillo, fully aware of Villa's reliance on trains, destroyed about 15 miles of rails between Torreon and Saltillo. Finding their advance obstructed, General Angeles suggested to Villa that they send their 8,000-strong cavalry to attack the town of Paredon. This town was the first line of defense protecting Saltillo with some 5,000 federal troops. The town was practically isolated since General Pablo Gonzalez's Division of the Northeast was blocking the town's link to the north. Angeles suggested mobilizing an additional 2,000 troops to block their potential withdrawal to the south and force them to move to Saltillo where they could engage the 8,000 additional federal forces stationed there.

Angeles's plan was to weaken the federal forces before engaging them at Saltillo. This proved to be an excellent strategy. Perhaps because of its isolated condition, the federal army at Paredon was defeated before even engaging Villa. The federal forces had hoped that disabling the train tracks was enough to dissuade Villa from attacking this town. For this reason, they did not conduct the required scouting missions to follow Villa's movement and they were taken completely by surprise. Their defenses fell almost immediately, turning into a disorderly retreat. The Villistas managed to blow up the escaping locomotive and engage the desperate federal army. Hundreds began to surrender hoping for clemency, while others shed their uniforms trying to escape disguised as peasants. The Villistas' morale soared. Villa was now ready to assault Saltillo with an additional 10 cannons and 3,000 rifles, and 100 additional troops consisting of defecting soldiers from the federal army. The officers, as usual, were summarily executed.

Villa's strength was so impressive that the battle at Saltillo never took place. The terrified and isolated garrison decided to abandon the city before the Villistas arrived. The federal soldiers destroyed their artillery and weapons, set fire to buildings, and looted the city in order keep its supplies and resources from the revolutionaries. To Carranza's dismay, Villa's occupation of Saltillo consolidated his reputation of invincibility. By most accounts, the Division of the North had become the most formidable army ever produced by the revolution.

Natera's Failure at Zacatecas

As Villa consolidated another triumph at Saltillo the revolutionaries in Zacatecas were encountering fearless resistance from the federal forces. General Natera and his Army of the Center were no match for Huerta's strong defenses. Following the Villista tradition, Natera had launched continuous infantry attacks supported by cavalry charges, but Zacatecas's geography favored the defenders. The city lay in a valley sheltered by two hills, El Grillo and La Bufa, perfectly located to place defensive artillery. Carranza was forced to consider calling Villa to help him conquer Zacatecas.

Villa's Resignation

Fearing the political implication of Villa's rising star, Carranza seriously considered calling the Division of the North to Zacatecas. He first ordered Villa to stay at Saltillo and send 3,000 troops to assist Natera. Soon after he reconsidered and asked Villa to send instead 5,000 soldiers. Villa was furious. He was well aware that Carranza needed him, but was determined to keep him from succeeding in Zacatecas. For the first time, he seriously considered disobeying the First Chief. He hesitated. Instead of becoming a rebel, he decided to throw in the towel and telegraphed Carranza his resignation. Carranza was delighted. He could count on Villa's superior army without his political liability. Without hesitation the First Chief accepted it.

Unexpectedly, perhaps to everybody, Villa's resignation consolidated him as the most important leader of the revolution. In accepting Villa's resignation, Carranza overlooked its political effect on the Division of the North. Without Villa, his generals were forced to mobilize to Zacatecas and place themselves under the command of General Natera. Apart from the respect that they had for Villa, many of these generals were more experienced and successful than Natera and found this situation insulting.

Led by General Angeles, the generals of the Division of the North protested Carranza's decision. They threatened Carranza, indicating that they would only remain in the army if Villa stayed. They also tried to convince Villa to reconsider and remain at the head of their army. This situation emboldened Villa. He now was certain that his generals would follow him if he decided to break away from Carranza.

Villa's Political Independence from Carranza

Villa found himself in a stronger political position and tried to capitalize on it. He took his conflict with Carranza to a new level. He began creating political alliances with different groups throughout the country. He approached Emiliano Zapata and Governor Jose Maria Maytorena, who he knew did not trust Carranza. Zapata, the peasant leader of the Liberation Army of the South, was an open supporter of Villa's land confiscations conducted in Chihuahua. He believed that Carranza, an aristocratic landowner, was not a real revolutionary. Governor Maytorena shared Carranza's social policies which antagonized Zapata. However, he disliked Carranza for his political interference in his state: Sonora. Villa tried to form with them a second revolutionary front challenging Carranza's authority.

Villa was emerging as the political leader of a strong revolutionary coalition independent from Carranza. The moment had come to openly challenge Carranza's authority. Being careful not to suggest an open rebellion against the First Chief, Villa announced that he was ready to personally attack Zacatecas. Carranza had practically no alternative so he did not object.

THE BATTLE OF ZACATECAS

Villa knew full well that his political future could possibly depend on his victory at Zacatecas. This was not an easy challenge. Natera's failure had demonstrated that the geography of the city of Zacatecas made achieving a victory difficult. El Grillo and La Bufa formed two natural towers protecting Huerta's army. In addition, the surrounding area featured lower hills and was reinforced with trenches, barbed wires, and scattered wall structures that further complicated the advances of the large cavalry charges that were a regular part of Villa's strategy.

Huerta understood the importance of Zacatecas so decided to reinforce it as much as possible. General Luis Medina received 10,000 soldiers for its defense. As Villa approached the city, General Medina reinforced the hills with 12 artillery pieces and a generous supply of grenades and machine guns. He was determined to cause as many casualties as possible. He took into consideration the federal's successful defense at Ciudad Chihuahua. He made arrangements, hoping that he could resist five days of attacks and demoralize the Villistas. In addition, this extra time would allow the mobilization of 15,000 additional troops from Aguascalientes. He expected that this massive reinforcement would be sufficient to completely destroy Villa.

Regardless of all these advantages, not everything favored General Medina. His troops, although numerous, lacked proper supplies, arms, and food. As Villa besieged the city on June 16, anxiety plagued the defenders. They were forced to ration food and limit their engagement with the enemy in order to save ammunition. Anxiety grew as they saw an endless flow of Villistas arriving in revolutionary trains. After a few days Villa had mobilized close to 20,000 troops and had 39 cannon. The military force that Villa fielded was also alarming Carranza.

Villa's Strategy

As preparations to attack Zacatecas were taking place, Villa remained for a few extra days at Torreon. He was securing the flow of supplies from

Chihuahua and dealing with Carranza's envoys who were attempting to bring Villa under Carranza's command. In the meantime at Zacatecas, General Angeles studied possible strategies while sending scouts to gather intelligence. Angeles convincingly suggested to Villa that without the destruction of the defensive artillery Zacatecas could not be conquered. He suggested not engaging on frontal attacks, as Natera had done, but using artillery with two specific goals in mind: protect the advancing troops and destroy the defensive artillery the federal forces had placed at the hill tops.

Nervous Skirmishes

Between June 19 and 23, as the Villistas continued arriving and assuming offensive positions, brief skirmishes took place. Tension was growing on both sides and occasionally soldiers shot nervously whenever the enemy showed its presence. Sometimes the opposite side responded in kind, but officers on both sides insisted on holding fire. Villa was still in Torreon and had given strict orders not to engage before he could assess the situation and personally lead the attack. Villa, however, did not let anybody know when he could be expected so impatience ran high.

On June 21, one particular skirmish came close to a full-blown battle. An artillery shell struck the battalion of revolutionary general Maclovio Herrera, killing three of his men. Tired of waiting for Villa, Herrera pulled out his pistol and led a charge. As he approached the city from the south, the federal forces' machine guns and artillery caused high casualties. Seeing this, Generals Chao and Angeles sent their troops to save Herrera's men. The federal army was under the impression that the attack on the city had finally begun. By the end of the day the Villistas retreated to their original positions and tried to cool down their anxiety. The federal troops had the sense that they had contained the attack and their morale improved. The next day was a quiet one—the calm before the storm.

On June 22, Villa finally made his way to Zacatecas. After supervising all the battalions and discussing Angeles's strategy, he decided on a simultaneous attack from four fronts (north, south, southeast, and southwest).

The Attack

The attack on Zacatecas began from all fronts at 10:00 A.M. on June 25, 1914. Angeles was using his artillery effectively, protecting the advancing forces from the north. The poorly supplied federal forces at Loreto Hill, one of the first lines of defense, were pounded by shells and threatened by rapidly advancing infantry. After 25 minutes the federal forces were unable to contain the advance and abandoned the hill. Angeles could now move his artillery to a better position to attack the strategically important El Grillo Hill. On the opposite front, the federal army's artillery was ineffective, often aiming too high. A Villista brigade led by Raul Madero stormed El Grillo, but its defenses resisted, forcing him to halt the assault. An artillery exchange followed, as both sides tried to gain some advantage. At about 1:00 P.M., Villistas tried another attack on El Grillo. This time, Villa's troops were in an excellent position for a direct attack on the hill while troops led by General Natera from the south were successfully filtering into Zacatecas.

Suddenly a huge explosion shocked the city. The weapons depot had been blown up. It is not clear what caused the explosion. Some people believed that Villistas did it accidentally by shooting as they stormed the building. Others believed that federal officers ordered the explosion as a last heroic act. The fact is that the depot exploded as Natera's troops were entering the building. The result: 37 Villistas, 89 federal troops, and 9 civilians, from the building next door, killed.

As Villistas reinforced their attack on El Grillo Hill, the federal forces there lost their nerve, panicked, and fled. By 4:30 that afternoon, Villista flags crowned all the defensive hills surrounding Zacatecas. The city was now the main battleground, resulting in enormous death and destruction. A hail of bullets killed not only soldiers but also a large number of civilians and horses, complicating the mobility of Villistas in the streets. A large group of federal forces tried to escape to the south, but General Natera, who was blocking that exit, intercepted and destroyed them. Back in the city, federal soldiers began storming houses and stores trying to find civilian clothing to avoid capture. Finally, at 5:35 that evening, Zacatecas fell under Villa's control.

Although brief, the Battle of Zacatecas was the deadliest battle of the entire second phase of the revolution. In approximately eight hours of battle, "6,000 federals and 1,000 of Villa's soldiers had died, 3,000 federals and 2,000 of Villa's soldiers had been wounded, and a large number of civilians had been injured or killed."[1]

Villa in Zacatecas

After Zacatecas was under control, Villa forbade looting and any act of violence. As became typical of Villa's army, all consumption of alcohol was forbidden. In the aftermath of the attack, Villa found Zacatecas in shatters, a large number of buildings destroyed or showing signs of intense street fighting; dead bodies everywhere. He ordered 3,000 prisoners to begin cleaning the city and digging graves. In the meantime, Huerta loyalists were executed. Villa had no problem incorporating most regular soldiers into his victorious army. Villa specifically ordered his soldiers not to execute anyone with artillery expertise.

Zacatecas was Villa's most important triumph of his career. Villa had swung open the door for the revolution to enter triumphantly the country's capital. Nothing, it seemed, could stop Villa from taking Mexico City and capturing Huerta.

Villa Stopped in His Tracks

Villa's success at Zacatecas after bypassing Carranza's authority was a major blow to the latter's claim as the First Chief of the revolution. Carranza's last hope was to keep Villa from entering Mexico City. Simply ordering him to stop would not do. Villa had demonstrated a dangerous level of independence and willingness to disobey the First Chief. Carranza decided to make use of his control over the coal mines of Durango to stop Villa in his tracks. Villa depended on this coal to power his trains. Carranza's order made it impossible for Villa to move further south.

President Wilson's Change of Heart

In order to circumvent Carranza, Villa could have bought coal from the United States, but to his dismay President Wilson decreed an embargo of arms and resources to all Villa-controlled territories. This was not an act against the revolution. The U.S. president did not do the same to Carranza. This policy appears counterintuitive to President Wilson's favorable opinion toward Villa and his serious concerns regarding Carranza's uncompromising nationalism. President Wilson was interested in mediating among all the warring factions, something that Villa's overwhelming victories would have made irrelevant. Without coal from the United States, Villa had no alternative but to retreat north, back to Torreon, and let Carranza take Mexico City.

THE FALL OF HUERTA

After Zacatecas, Huerta understood that a revolutionary triumph was a matter of days. On July 15, Huerta's 17-month-old dictatorship came to an abrupt end. He resigned and with the protection of 600 soldiers fled Mexico City to the port of Veracruz where he sailed to his exile in Spain. The federal forces, in a desperate act of survival, offered their services simultaneously to Carranza, Villa, and Zapata. They hoped that they could provide an additional advantage to one of these factions and thus land on the victorious side of a divided revolution. However, none of the revolutionary leaders was interested in an alliance with the federal army.

Villa understood that, even though he had achieved the most important victories of the revolution against Huerta, he would not be the conqueror of Mexico City. This honor would be granted by Carranza to General Alvaro Obregon. A month after Huerta's resignation, Obregon entered Mexico City after having negotiated the surrender of the federal army in the nearby town of Teoloyucan. Carranza was now in control of the revolution and the country. Villa had been outsmarted.

The Fiasco at Niagara Falls

President Wilson tried to influence developments in Mexico by inviting representatives of the various factions of the conflict to discuss a negotiated peace agreement at Niagara Falls. His principle goal was to salvage as much as possible the existing structures of power in order to avoid anarchy while helping create a more democratic government in which neither Villa nor Carranza could monopolize power. However, the Niagara Falls meeting was a failure. The revolutionary factions sent observers, but not official representatives, refusing to commit to any agreement orchestrated by the U.S. government.

ONE REVOLUTION, TWO LEADERS

Typically in revolutions, once the common enemy is destroyed revolutionaries fight among themselves to secure their own power, forgetting the goals that inspired the revolution in the first place. The revolution had lost Madero who, regardless of his faults, was considered by most the legitimate leader of the revolution. Carranza tried to replace him and to some degree succeeded. However, he lacked charisma and not even Carranza's most loyal generals considered him the commander in chief. Indeed, Carranza had no real control over most of the military forces that were fighting for him. Often he was forced to tolerate the independence of his generals and could only command them whenever he was able to co-opt them by becoming their provider of money, weapons, food, railroads, and so forth.

Among all revolutionary leaders Villa was the strongest and the most independent. His own access to resources from Chihuahua and the United States allowed him to cover most of his needs. After Huerta's defeat both Villa and Carranza claimed the leadership of the revolution. However, neither one could claim total control of the nation. Carranza had Mexico City, but Villa still commanded the most powerful army in the country. To complicate matters more, other generals, especially General Obregon, began contemplating leading the revolution.

This stalemate was primarily a problem of egos. Both Villa and Carranza thought that they were more competent and the rightful leader of the revolution. However, leadership is a complex and multidimensional phenomenon that requires not only big egos, but also the ability to attract a wide range of supporters, something that both were very good at doing, which increased the division within the revolution and the possibility of a civil war.

Competing Revolutionary Agendas

The conflict between Villa and Carranza was also a struggle to define the Mexico that would emerge from the revolution. Carranza advocated for a civilian administration with a centralized government directing national politics and policies from Mexico City. He considered this indispensable to overpower local strongmen and secure peace, stability, and democracy. He refused to enact drastic social reforms such as widespread distribution of lands to poor peasants or workers' right to unionize and strike. He suggested that social policies had to be addressed by the notion of equality before the law and emphasized the protection of private property.

Villa offered an opposite vision for a postrevolutionary Mexico. In addition to his communes, he advocated for a weak central government and strengthening local and regional governments. Thus, democracy would not be orchestrated from Mexico City, but from local and regional officials electing their representatives to the capital of the country. Villa's social policies were somehow vague, but he clearly favored a form of welfare state.

Villistas and Carrancistas each disliked the other's model so much that reconciliation was increasingly impossible. For Villistas, Carranza's centralized model guaranteed the permanence of the status quo under a new dictator. For Carrancistas, Villa's model represented anarchy and economic decline. Many others, being more practical, supported either one according to whom they considered was the most likely to emerge as the leader of the revolution.

Revolutionary Leaders Begin Taking Sides

In the months following the fall of Huerta, different factions lobbied, negotiated, and shifted loyalties depending on who offered better opportunities to advance their own interests. Several attempts were made between July and December 1914 to solve this political impasse. All efforts failed and before the year's end the revolutionaries turned their guns against each other. This third phase of the revolution was the bloodiest of all.

In the wake of this political division, the country was divided into five military regions. At this point, Villa commanded the most successful, largest, most powerful, better organized, and best supplied of all revolutionary armies: the Division of the North. Villa's headquarters were located at Ciudad Chihuahua. Emiliano Zapata led a conglomerate of peasant militias in south-central Mexico known as the Liberation Army of the South. His headquarters were in the state of Morelos, just south of Mexico City. Panfilo Natera, a Villista appointed by Carranza, commanded the Division of the Center. His base was in Aguascalientes. Perhaps the most powerful leader after Villa was Carrancista General Pablo Gonzalez, leader of the Division of the Northeast based in Tamaulipas—an oil-rich territory. The fifth region was the Northwest, commanded by General Alvaro Obregon, perhaps the most astute politician of all the generals. His headquarters were at Hermosillo, Sonora.

General Alvaro Obregon as a Third Alternative

General Alvaro Obregon was a rising star. Unlike Villa's Chihuahua, his home state of Sonora was poor and isolated so he depended heavily on Carranza's resources. Obregon shared Carranza's ambition for national power more than any of the five major military leaders, including Villa. Obregon orchestrated the surrender of the federal army at Teoloyucan, which placed him in the national spotlight, and he was determined to make the most out of it. He suggested that he could become a neutral leader, an alternative to Villa and Carranza. However, Obregon was no competition to Carranza's and Villa's power and popularity.

The Conference of Torreon

One of the first efforts to avoid civil war took place at Torreon: a conference of representatives of the various factions of the revolution. It was organized by the Carrancista General Pablo Gonzalez. Rather than generating consensus, his goal was to consolidate Carranza's political position by weakening Villa's military influence. On July 5 and 6 they met and signed an agreement under which Villa would recognize Carranza as the First Chief of the revolution and Carranza would recognize Villa as the leader of the Division of the North and send him coal, arms, and supplies. They also discussed defining the direction of the revolution. Unlike Madero's insistence on regaining the confidence of the federal army, the attendees agreed to dissolve the federal army and replace it with a unified revolutionary army. The Catholic Church, considered a major supporter of Huerta's dictatorship, was banned from any political activity. The conference also agreed to prioritize social reforms with an emphasis on the welfare of peasants and workers. Many people at Torreon believed they had averted civil war and unified the revolution.

The declaration at Torreon was instead a fiasco. Villa refused to accept any resolution that recognized Carranza as the head of the revolution and Carranza refused to lift the coal embargo, his only source of effective power over Villa. In addition, the declaration proposed a radical social agenda that Carranza thought disastrous for agricultural and industrial productivity. Like Madero, Carranza believed that social reforms should be gradual in order to improve the condition of the poor, but without affecting the interests of the wealthy. Both Villa and Carranza refused to accept the results of the conference.

Villa Tries to Replace Carranza

Villa tried to find a rival politician who, like Carranza, could claim legitimacy by having been elected during Madero's presidency. He considered Jose Maria Maytorena, the governor of Sonora. Following Huerta's coup, Maytorena did not confront Huerta. Rather he left a deputy governor before fleeing to the United States. Maytorena only returned to resume his governorship after General Obregon had expelled the federal army from Sonora. Many considered him a coward so he couldn't claim Carranza's leadership and courage, much less the leadership of the revolution.

Villa offered military support to Governor Maytorena, helping him consolidate his power in the state and reduce his dependency on Obregon. Maytorena's dependency on Villa's forces, Villa reasoned, would secure Villa's influence on a Maytorena government.

Obregon Joining Forces with Villa

For his part, General Alvaro Obregon continued styling himself as a third alternative to Villa and Carranza. He was well aware of Villa's power and national charisma. Thus, rather than confront him, Obregon tried to manipulate him. In early September 1914 he contacted Villa and arranged for a face-to-face meeting in Chihuahua. By proposing the meeting in Villa's home territory, Obregon was trying to gain his trust by putting himself at Villa's mercy. He reminded Villa that they represented the two most powerful armies so they could easily control the entire country. This alliance appealed to Villa. Obregon's only demand was to retain his power in Sonora by keeping Maytorena dependent on his army. In reality, they both needed each other to accomplish their respective goals.

During the meeting with Obregon, Villa agreed not to support Maytorena, but with some conditions. He requested that Generals Plutarco E. Calles and Bernardo Hill, who were in charge of Obregon's troops in Sonora, be transferred to Chihuahua and that Juan Cabral, a weak politician that Villa expected to manipulate, be named governor of Sonora. In addition, he requested Obregon not recognize Carranza as First Chief. The negotiations were meant to fail. Placing his best generals under Villa would have made Obregon completely dependent on him so Obregon refused. Nevertheless, even if Obregon had agreed, it is unlikely that Maytorena, Calles, or Hill would have supported such an agreement.

Villa Orders Obregon's Execution

Despite the failed negotiation, Villa invited Obregon to join him to celebrate the approaching anniversary of Mexican independence in Ciudad Chihuahua. Obregon was interested in continuing talks with Villa so he accepted. He began secret talks with Villa's generals in order to assess the possibility of attracting them to his side. He approached particularly those generals who cherished their political independence and those who were not prepared to support Villa's attempt to break with Carranza and risk a civil war.

Villa soon became suspicious of Obregon's activities in Chihuahua. He also was angry because Obregon did not condemn Carranza's candidacy for the upcoming presidential election. Furthermore, Villa received a telegram indicating that General Hill was attacking Maytorena's forces in Sonora. Villa was outraged and ordered Obregon to stop the conflict, but Obregon explained that he could not stop it. Villa considered this proof of Obregon's treacherous intentions and confronted him. Soon they began exchanging insults, and witnesses were afraid that they would begin shooting at each other. Driven by his explosive personality, Villa ended the dispute by ordering Obregon's arrest and execution. Many people thought this was a big mistake and tried to persuade him against it. Luz Corral, Villa's wife, told him that he would go down in history as the man who did not respect the sacredness of hospitality. Roque Gonzalez Garza insisted that Carranza would use this execution to convince many that Villa was in fact nothing more than a bloodthirsty bandit. Felipe Angeles also intervened and managed to convince Villa to stop the execution.[2] However harsh Villa's position may have appeared, it was not completely out of place. He clearly understood that if his conflict with Carranza turned into a civil war, Obregon might become his most formidable opponent and it was easier to nip a probable enemy in the bud. Regardless, he conceded and halted the execution. He regretted this decision the following year while in the midst of the civil war.

The Conference in Mexico City

While Obregon was risking his life for political gain, Carranza was doing his part to be recognized as the presidential candidate of the revolution. For this purpose, on October 1 he organized a meeting of governors and generals in Mexico City. In order to guarantee his desired outcome, he had carefully handpicked the representatives. They were mainly civilian politicians. Most of them were either known Carrancistas or leaders against a possible conflict between revolutionary forces.

This conference did nothing to solve the real impasse because Villa did not recognize the meeting. He insisted that representatives of the revolution could not be simple politicians, but rather each one of them should represent 1,000 soldiers. Since Villa was the commander of the largest Mexican army at the time, this would have guaranteed that the larger number of representatives would be Villistas. Carranza insisted that, since the purpose of the meeting was to restructure the political order in Mexico, the meeting should be strictly civilian. In any event, Villa refused to recognize the legitimacy of this meeting and Emiliano Zapata, who did not trust Carranza, also refused.

Since the meeting in Mexico City brought together most of the Carrancista hierarchy, Carranza feared that Villa could easily destroy Carrancismo if he decided to attack. As a precaution he ordered the train tracks connecting Torreon and Zacatecas destroyed, leaving Villa unable to move south. Villa was outraged and, on September 24, he made his first public statement indicating that he no longer recognized Carranza as the First Chief of the revolution.

At this point, Obregon, who had just narrowly escaped Villa's firing squad, was leaving Chihuahua headed for Mexico City. Villa's breakup with Carranza meant an imminent civil war. In an attempt to destroy Carranza's military hierarchy, Villa once again ordered the detention and execution of Obregon. Luckily for Obregon, some of Villa's generals, who had been conspiring with Obregon, arrived at the train station where he was detained and set him free.

Many revolutionary leaders expressed their concern regarding Villa's breakup with Carranza. At least 50 of Carranza's generals, including Obregon, tried to keep Villa from escalating their differences into a civil war. They also suggested that Carranza should withdraw his candidacy for the presidency.

Carranza argued that, according to the constitution, military officers had no authority to remove him from power. He insisted that it was only during extraordinary circumstances, such as Huerta's coup, that a representative assembly of elected officials could elect the chief executive of the country. Military officials were purposely kept from this process in order to avoid the military overpowering the rule of law. Indeed, governors and other elected officials met at Mexico City to support Carranza's right to the presidency. However, civilian leaders were concerned that such confirmation practically guaranteed the dreaded civil war. Thus, during their gathering they recognized that under the circumstances the next revolutionary president must be recognized by both civilian and military leaders of the revolution. This resolution failed to solve the impasse.

The assembly of elected representatives in Mexico City agreed that there was a pressing need for a more comprehensive convention, one including representatives from the most important military and civilian revolutionary factions and whose primary goal was to elect their revolutionary president. Thus, a general convention was announced for October 5 at the city of Aguascalientes.

All groups concerned responded positively, except for Zapata and Carranza. After his experience with Madero, Zapata stopped trusting politicians and decided to continue his struggle alone. Carranza, for his part, refused to recognize any political agreement dominated by military officers. He remained in Mexico City and refused to send representatives.

THE CONVENTION OF AGUASCALIENTES

The convention of Aguascalientes was Carranza's most serious challenge to his presidential ambitions. He was respected by his fellow politicians, but not by most military officers, including many of his own generals. Villa expected to dominate the convention because the military delegates were the most numerous.

Threatened by Villa's potential success at Aguascalientes, Carranza, once again, made use of the Mexican constitution to indicate that only a civilian government could make political decisions and that the military elements of the revolution should be subordinated to such government.

The problem with Carranza's argument was that the structures of civilian power considered by the constitution had been weakened by Huerta's coup and practically destroyed by the war that followed. Carranza may have had the law on his side, but the new revolutionary reality was that the revolutionary army had become the major tool for political legitimacy. Indeed, the representatives at the convention of Aguascalientes were mostly military officers. However, they represented many and disparate factions so that neither Villa nor Carranza was able to dominate the convention.

This event was also vital for Villa's political success. In order to gain enough advantage he continued insisting that each delegate must represent 1,000 soldiers. However, most delegates of other factions were concerned about an overwhelming Villista presence, and while they never openly rejected Villa's idea, it was never implemented. At the beginning of the convention there were a total of 152 delegates and only 35 of them were representatives of the Division of the North.[3] In the end, Villa's faction was influential but not dominant.

General Obregon tried to manipulate the convention by promoting the idea that the only way to secure a peaceful solution was getting rid of both Villa and Carranza. He was promoting his candidacy as an ideal alternative. In addition, he suggested that in order to avoid a civil war caused by unsatisfied parties, all delegates had to sign a Mexican flag as proof of their commitment and respect for the convention's resolution. Most agreed and signed the flag.

No Revolutionary Policies

The convention became a sort of political musical chairs, but this month-long convention was, in terms of framing the policies and goals of the revolution, fairly irrelevant. Many representatives supported one leader or another depending on the possibility of a position in the forming government. Speeches reminded the audience about the need for social reform, including better rights for workers and peasants, as well as political reform, primarily the establishment of a fair and legitimate democratic system. However, no specific steps to achieve such goals were ever discussed. The main breakthrough at the convention, in terms of policy, happened at the end of October, when Felipe Angeles and other Villistas managed to convince Zapata to send delegates to the convention. Zapata agreed only after the convention guaranteed that his plan for land reform would be included in the final resolution. Once Zapata's 26 delegates arrived the convention could claim to represent all factions of the revolution. As such, most delegates believed that the convention could avert the civil war.

Villa's Goal: A Revolution Without Carranza

Nevertheless, Villa and Carranza continued threatening the success of the convention. At the convention hardliner Villistas and Carrancistas engaged in diatribes against their opponents. Many agreed with Obregon's idea of removing both Villa and Carranza to avoid civil war.

Villa decided to increase his influence on the debate by personally assisting and addressing the delegates. He arrived on October 16 and as a gesture of good faith he signed the resolution-binding ceremonial flag. In his speech, Villa assured the delegates that he had no political ambitions. He was not interested in assuming any political office, much less the presidency. He declared that he was only interested in remaining at the head of the Division of the North, solely to guarantee that Carranza never become president of Mexico. Many Carrancistas were outraged and some yelled their desire to kill him on the spot.

A Plot to Kill Villa

Afraid of Villa's potential success at Aguascalientes, Carrancistas made at least one serious attempt to assassinate him. This plot was masterminded by General Pablo Gonzalez. The chosen assassin was an obscure individual from Argentina, Francisco L. Mugica, known as "El Gaucho." He had fled Argentina after killing two people. In Mexico, he worked in a circus where he killed a third individual and was sent to prison. He escaped during Huerta's coup after artillery destroyed one of the prison's walls. He joined the revolution and was again imprisoned. Finally, he was freed when Obregon claimed Mexico City in the name of the revolution. "El Gaucho" managed to gain Villa's trust, out of sympathy and admiration for his turbulent past. While working for Villa, he visited a prison in Mexico City. Villista prisoners learned that during this visit the chief of police paid "El Gaucho" to kill Villa. Villa investigated and confirmed that General Pablo Gonzalez was behind this plot. After "El Gaucho" returned, Villa confronted him and smacked him across the face with his gun. "El Gaucho" was executed soon after.[4]

Neither Villa Nor Carranza

By early November, the tension between Villa and Carranza had reached a boiling point. The convention finally agreed to send commissions to convince them both that they had to leave the country for the sake of the revolution. Villa, perhaps aware that Carranza would not accept such a proposition, declared at the convention that he was prepared to leave if Carranza promised to do the same. Carranza declared that, while he did not recognize the authority of the convention, he would accept its proposition if both Villa and Zapata left their armies.

The convention agreed to formally request that Villa and Carranza leave Mexico. Villa, in a melodramatic stand, sent a letter to the convention insisting that he and Carranza should be executed for the good of the country. However, he insisted that he would only surrender himself if Carranza agreed to do the same, which, of course, Carranza did not.

In the meantime, the convention moved ahead to elect an interim president that all factions could support. Electing Villa or Carranza meant a possible civil war, so Obregon was proposed as the safest candidate. However, perhaps in reaction to the many problems caused by the powerful revolutionary leaders, the convention decided to elect a weak and obscure regional leader. General Eulalio Gutierrez, the commander of a relatively small militia in San Luis Potosi, was declared president of Mexico. They considered that his lack of power prevented him from overpowering other factions and becoming a new dictator. Most delegates were satisfied. They thought that they had found a perfect solution to unite the revolution.

Carranza Refuses to Recognize the Convention's Resolution

After the election of President Gutierrez, Carranza realized his declining power and his vulnerable position in Mexico City. He announced his plan to go sightseeing to the pre-Columbian ruins of Teotihuacan, but this was only an excuse to flee Mexico City and establish his headquarters in the port of Veracruz. Obregon was appointed by the convention to reach Carranza and convince him to accept its resolution. He told Carranza that President Gutierrez gave him until November 10 to announce his submission to the new government. Carranza argued that a country led by military generals would only perpetuate the cycle of violence. It was him, he declared, and not General Gutierrez, who represented the best hope to pacify Mexico. He refused to recognize the legitimacy of the new president. In response, President Gutierrez declared him in rebellion and ordered his arrest. President Gutierrez appointed Villa head of the Convencionista army in charge of capturing Carranza and his supporters. Obregon became outraged that Villa received such a prominent role and decided to join Carranza.

The Convention of Aguascalientes was organized first and foremost to resolve the quarrels between Villa and Carranza, but it failed. President Gutierrez, without an army of his own, depended completely on Villa's strength. Carrancistas and other anti-Villistas united their forces to challenge Villa. By November 5, 1914, the Convencionsitas (Villistas) and the Constitucionalistas (Carrancistas) announced the beginning of hostilities. The third phase of the revolution had begun. Between 1914 and 1915, this fratricidal war became the bloodiest period of the entire Mexican Revolution.

NOTES

1. Friedrich Katz, *The Life and Times of Pancho Villa* (Stanford, CA: Stanford University Press, 1998), 353.

2. Paco Ignacio Taibo II, *Pancho Villa: Una biografía narrativa* (Mexico: Editorial Planeta, 2006), 414.

3. Katz, *Life and Times of Pancho Villa*, 424.

4. Taibo, *Pancho Villa*, 431.

Chapter 5

NEVER GIVE UP (1915–1916)

The Convention of Aguascalientes failed at its most urgent goal: uniting all revolutionaries behind a single leader to avoid a civil war. The main reason for this was that the revolution was not a single movement. Rather, it was a conglomerate of local, regional, and national leaders representing practically all social classes and a variety of geographic interests. Only Pancho Villa and Venustiano Carranza possessed enough national appeal and power to unite these disparate groups, but their rivalry only succeeded at creating two antagonistic camps. The selection of a weak president by the convention complicated the situation further. The new president, Eulalio Gutierrez, did not have any real power and found himself unable to control Villa and Carranza. The result of all this was the bloodiest phase of the revolution.

THE STORM AFTER AGUASCALIENTES

On November 10, 1914, Carranza defied President Gutierrez's order to comply with the Resolution of Aguascalientes, so Pancho Villa, as head of the Convencionista army, was commissioned to capture Carranza—an event some consider the official start of the civil war. However, the first few weeks that followed saw practically no battlefield action. It was a period in which the various factions of the revolution were trying to decide which side to join. For instance, Zapata identified himself with Villa's humble origins, his commitment to the poor, and his mistrust for Carranza. Not surprisingly, he joined the Convencionistas. Another important general, Pablo Gonzalez, remained with the First Chief. Unexpectedly, however, as soon as he announced his decision, his Division of the Northeast began to fall apart. Desertions ran rampant as many of his officers decided to leave with their men and join Villa. Gonzalez left Mexico City with 20,000 men, but by the time he finally arrived at his headquarters in Tampico he could count barely 3,000 of them.

General Obregon had failed at his attempt to emerge as the third presidential alternative at the convention so he was forced to take sides. Not even he respected the signing of the Mexican flag as a pledge among all factions to respect and support the convention's resolution. Instead, he joined Carranza. Perhaps Obregon thought he could enjoy a stronger position with Carranza, who was not a military man. Had he joined Villa, Obregon would have been his subordinate with limited influence in military matters. Furthermore, Carranza's policies protecting private property and a strong central government aligned more with Obregon's philosophy, as he was a middle-class farmer. At the same time, Obregon probably resented Villa for the way he had treated him in Chihuahua, twice condemning him to the firing squad.

The situation got more complicated when the United States decided to leave the port of Veracruz to Carranza, providing him with an important source of revenue from import-export taxes. Veracruz became an excellent gateway for supplying Carranza's need for resources. From the port he comfortably commanded his generals by controlling the distribution of resources needed for their military campaigns.

Regardless of Carranza's important gains during this period, Villa was the most powerful man in Mexico. He controlled a larger territory and counted far more and better armed troops. According to some estimates, Villa had some 60,000 troops while Carranza, at best, could count half that number. His territory ran from the U.S. border to Mexico City and from the Pacific coast to the Gulf of Mexico, with the exception of northern Sonora in the northwest and Tamaulipas in the northeast. His influence extended further south thanks to his alliance with Emiliano Zapata. In contrast, Carranza was in a precarious situation, cornered at Veracruz and having indirect influence in the isolated states of Tamaulipas and Sonora. He also claimed control over the Mexican southeast, but the Yucatan Peninsula played a limited role in the revolution.

The Strength of the Constitucionalistas

In December 1914, everything suggested that Carranza's fall would take place within a matter of days. However, there was some strength in the limited territory under his control. His territory enjoyed the most stable financial conditions. Tamaulipas and the Yucatan Peninsula contained the largest deposits of crude oil in the country. Furthermore, the Yucatan Peninsula was emerging as one of the largest global producers of sisal for the manufacturing of ropes. In August 1914, the demand for oil and ropes increased to supply the war efforts during World War I, generating handsome profits for Carranza. Complementing the natural resources of these regions, the ports of Tampico (in Tamaulipas) and Veracruz, two of the most important ports in the country, allowed a swift interconnection of Carranza's otherwise divided territory. As long as the United States did not block these ports, he could count on a steady flow of cash, weapons, and other supplies to fight the Convencionistas. In addition to his economic strength, he was promoting a national agenda that contrasted with Villa's and Zapata's regional programs. Carranza had considerable experience working in the federal government and was quite comfortable commanding his generals in a nationwide military campaign. He promised to create a new constitution that would transform the goals of the revolution into the law of the land.

THE ALLIANCE BETWEEN VILLA AND ZAPATA

Regardless of Carranza's strength, few people considered him capable of defeating Villa. Villa's power was demonstrated by the way he arrived at Mexico City. Not strong enough to fight Villa, General Pablo Gonzalez abandoned Mexico City as Villa's trains approached. The manner by which the Convencionista army entered the city suggests that Villa was indeed the most powerful man in the country. Even the other most popular leader of the revolution, Zapata, being closer to Mexico City, decided to wait for Villa. General Angeles was leading the Villista vanguard of the Convencionista forces, but he, too, waited for his leader in the outskirts of the city. In the meantime, President Gutierrez arrived at Mexico City and occupied his offices practically unnoticed by most Mexicans. Everybody in the capital anxiously awaited—some thrilled, some terrified—for the arrival of Villa, the legendary, unquestioned leader of the revolution.

Villa and Zapata Meet at Xochimilco

Before entering the capital, Villa and Zapata arranged to meet on December 4, 1914 at the village of Xochimilco. This was the first time the most popular leaders of the Mexican Revolution met face to face. Politically speaking, they were both simple men, but they were both extremely charismatic and successful leaders, perceived by millions as liberators of the poor and oppressed. As they stood in front of each other, they appeared ill at ease. They did not seem to know what to do. Shake hands? Embrace? They belonged to completely different regions and saw each other as foreigners wearing unfamiliar costumes. They opted for a handshake followed by an embrace and entered a house to talk about their campaign against Carranza. They did not know what to say and remained silent for some time. Their silence contrasted with the noise of firecrackers, yells, and whistles from those outside celebrating the historic meeting. Finally, Villa and Zapata began to speak, making awkward comments, but neither one knew how to reply. Zapata tried to lighten things up and offered cognac to Villa, unaware that he was not a drinker. Courteously, Villa made an unsuccessful attempt to drink from the glass placed in front of him. Somehow embarrassed, he asked instead for a glass of water.

After some time, Villa and Zapata finally found a topic that they both could relate to and talk passionately about: Carranza. They agreed that they had to stop him from becoming another dictator favoring the rich and oppressing the poor. It was clear that they had to join their forces and strike him at Veracruz before he could prepare his resistance, but they did not discuss any details about how to accomplish this task. Instead, Villa tried to impress Zapata by bragging about his great number of troops and seemingly endless supply of weapons and resources. Zapata became uncomfortable again and refused to talk about the strength of his army so they returned to their initial stage of uncomfortable silence.

Politically, Villa and Zapata shared important weaknesses that complicated the possibility of their emerging as victors of the revolution. Unlike Carranza, neither Villa nor Zapata was a national leader in the strict sense of the word. Certainly, they both had a broad national appeal, particularly among the masses. However, the nature of their power was regional not national. Zapata's forces consisted mainly of peasants closely linked to their villages, in which they divided their time between tilling the land and fighting the revolution. Thus, the Zapatista demand for land reform was regional in scope. Zapata fought for his communities in Morelos and the neighboring regions; he had no interest in sponsoring a national agenda.

In contrast, Villa's power and far-reaching military might suggested that he had the potential to be a national leader. However, on closer inspection, his political interests were mainly focused on Chihuahua and perhaps Durango. He fought for the rights and interests of the peoples of these states, and he did not really have a national agenda. Regardless of appearances, his military strength was also regional. It depended on staying in direct communication with the human, economic, and military resources coming from Chihuahua. Train lines were the umbilical cord keeping Villa alive beyond Chihuahua's borders. The farther he stretched his forces the weaker his vanguard became. Mexico as a whole was an abstract concept to most Villistas. They ventured beyond Chihuahua's borders only to defeat the dictator Huerta who had hijacked Chihuahuan politics. Their fatherland was Chihuahua and they considered themselves an occupying force in most of the territory under their control, especially Mexico City.

The Weakness of President Eulalio Gutierrez

Unfortunately for the Convencionistas, Villa's and Zapata's regional interests limited their ability to unite their armies and dominate the entire country, allowing Carranza some breathing space. They needed a national political leader who could unite and take advantage of their combined power. The obvious man was President Eulalio Gutierrez. However, he was elected president by the convention precisely because he was a weak leader. He enjoyed the legitimacy granted by the votes in Aguascalientes, but did not have any significant way to enforce his power in a country where guns had replaced the rule of law. He needed Villa and Zapata as much as Zapata and Villa needed him, but his generals did not understand this. In order for this alliance to function, Villa and Zapata had to subordinate their armies to the president. That never happened.

Villa and Zapata were suspicious of politicians and President Gutierrez was no exception. Zapata had been betrayed by both Madero and Carranza and felt that the main interest of most politicians was to exploit the poor and vulnerable. This belief weakened the likelihood that Villa and Zapata would work with the Convencionista president. Zapata highlighted this at Xochimilco when he told Villa: "I'll advise all our friends [i.e., politicians] to be very careful—if not, they will feel the blows of the machete . . . I am convinced that we shall not be fooled."[1]

Villa and Zapata both believed that they could handle the war against Carranza and emerge as the political leaders of the revolution while keeping their president on a short leash. This evolved into a self-defeating political strategy that began to unravel at Xochimilco. During their meeting, they did not talk about a national agenda or a comprehensive military campaign. They focused on controlling the president and criticizing Carranza. By not including President Gutierrez in this historic meeting, they implicitly agreed on the nature of their alliance. It was not a united army, but two separate armies offering mutual support. Villa promised to help Zapata attack Carranza at Veracruz by providing weapons and ammunition. Villa would concentrate on the isolated Carrancista strongholds in the northeast and northwest. Apart from that, there was no talk of coordinating their war efforts.

Villa and Zapata Take Formal Control of Mexico City

At the end of their historic if awkward meeting at Xochimilco, Villa and Zapata led a parade into Mexico City that most people prematurely considered a victory march. They were joined by thousands of cavalry troops. The well-dressed, disciplined, and armed Villistas contrasted with the ragged, undisciplined, and irregularly armed Zapatistas. Thousands of city dwellers observed the parade, some terrified by the idea of bandits taking over the city, some elated by the final triumph of the revolution. Some observers perhaps noticed that the nature of this parade symbolized the Convencionistas' reality: Villa and Zapata showed their power for everyone to see, while President Gutierrez was nowhere to be seen.

Nevertheless, Villa understood that the legitimacy of their struggle depended on the premise that they were defending President Gutierrez against the rebel Carranza. So, after a six-hour-long parade, Villa and Zapata went to the national palace to talk to President Gutierrez. On their way to the presidential office, another incident crystallized— in the minds of all national and foreign observers as well as in the minds of future generations—the power of these two leaders and the absence of their president. As they walked through the palace, Villa noticed some special chairs kept in a room. One chair in particular was rather ostentatious, the chair belonging to Emperor Maximilian of the Second Mexican Empire (1864–1867). This chair caught Villa's attention with its golden decoration that included the imperial eagle on the top of the back of the chair and feathered eagle feet on the chair's legs. Villa invited Zapata to sit, but the latter felt uncomfortable sitting on such a pretentious chair, perhaps sensing the corruptibility of power, and refused to sit on it. Villa showed no such bias; he jokingly sat on it and invited everybody to gather around for a picture (conveniently, journalists had been following them to report and photograph this historic day). Zapata sat to Villa's left on a less ornate chair. Villa was wearing the general's uniform and Zapata the charro suit they had worn in the parade. A couple of snapshots were taken showing Villa and Zapata surrounded by a motley crew of observers and supporters. The quick distribution of the pictures around the country and abroad made everybody believe that Villa had occupied the presidential chair and that Zapata was his lieutenant. The powerful images suggested that Villa and Zapata had taken formal control of the country. This photo became a powerful symbol of Villa's national power and his triumph over Carranza, a triumph yet to be accomplished.

A Crack in the Convencionista Unity

Regardless of all the meetings, festivities, and signs of unity between Zapatistas and Villistas, real division between these two forces emerged as soon as they settled down in Mexico City. This had less to do with Villa and Zapata and more to do with the violent members within their armies. Many soldiers who had committed grievances against one army were, or had become, members of the other. In particular, Villa's need for well-trained officers and artillerymen forced him to accept deserting members of the federal army, many of whom had committed atrocities against Zapatistas. Villa and Zapata at first tried to negotiate with some of these men, but without positive results as each leader tried to protect his own men. The soldiers, therefore, began taking justice into their own hands.

The highly acclaimed parade in which Villa's Division of the North and Zapata's Liberation Army of the South demonstrated the strength of their alliance was followed by several weeks of kidnappings and clandestine executions of members of these two armies. These attacks were not authorized by either of their leaders; Villa and Zapata were, at times, powerless or unwilling to stop the executions.

For example, Paulino Martinez had joined the anti-Villista elements at the convention. Villa had his own grievance against Martinez because Martinez had previously turned against President Madero and joined Orozco's rebellion. After Orozco's death, Martinez joined Zapata's army. After recognizing Martinez, Villistas kidnapped him, beat him to death, and then burned his body. His killing further strained the alliance between Villa and Zapata.

Violence only generated more violence and the situation got out of control. Both Zapatistas and Villistas expanded their hunt to include the Carrancistas who did not manage to leave the city. The already uneasy residents of the capital had their worst fears confirmed when they learned of the barbaric activities conducted by their uninvited guests.[2] During three weeks in December, Convencionistas killed about 150 people, most of them quietly at night.

The Targeting of Presidential Appointees

Not even members of President Gutierrez's government were immune to this hunt. For instance, Minister of Education Jose Vasconcelos, an outspoken critic of Villa and Zapata, was forced to leave the city as soon as he heard that they were looking for him. Particularly damaging for the Convencionista alliance were the executions of Guillermo Garcia Aragon and David Berlanga. These killings forced President Gutierrez to make public denouncements against Villa and Zapata, and he began considering ways to replace these generals.

Guillermo Garcia Aragon began his revolutionary career as a Zapatista, but he joined Madero when the latter became president. After Madero's assassination, Garcia Aragon joined Huerta's government. Shamelessly, he later rejoined the revolution when Huerta's defeat was imminent. Obviously, Zapata felt betrayed and resented Garcia Aragon for apparently always switching to the winning side. Garcia Aragon had become vice president of the convention, where Eulalio Gutierrez invited him to work for him as the governor of the National Palace (the presidential offices). During the reception that President Gutierrez gave to Villa and Zapata, the latter spotted Garcia Aragon, expressing his disapproval of his presence there. The next day, Garcia Aragon's family complained to the president that Zapatistas had kidnapped him, but the president was powerless. Garcia Aragon had already been court-martialed and executed.

This assassination came just before the killing of David Berlanga. He had been an outspoken member of the convention and showed particular contempt toward the popular elements of the revolution and particularly toward Villa and Zapata. In his diatribes, Berlanga reinforced the argument that Villa was no more than a bloodthirsty bandit, and Villa hated him for that. Berlanga supported the Convencionistas because he was trying to help President Gutierrez to gear the revolution toward a well-organized program of social and political reforms; he believed that Villa and Zapata were leading the revolution on a suicidal path of chaos and anarchy. In early December, he went to Mexico City to talk to the president as a representative of the Aguascalientes government. His contempt for Villistas was exposed once more when at the restaurant Sylvain he noticed that some Villistas refused to pay their bill. Outraged, Berlanga scolded the Villistas for their behavior and called them robbers and bandits. The Villistas decided not to tolerate more of his insults. The next day Rodolfo Fierro arrested him and soon after killed him. Berlanga showed so much courage facing his executioners it is said that Fierro regretted executing such a brave man. In any event, it is unclear if Fierro followed Villa's orders or acted on his own.[3]

This wave of violence did not help Villa's efforts to prove wrong those who described him as a bloodthirsty bandit. Carranza's propaganda machine took advantage of this and made the point that this wave of violence revealed the real Villa. Carranza even refused to call him Villa. Instead, Carranza referred to him by his original name, Doroteo Arango, to indicate that the image of the hero Pancho Villa was only a masquerade hiding the real bandit.

The murderous events in Mexico City seemed to prove Carranza's propaganda. For three weeks, Villistas killed Zapatistas, Zapatistas killed Villistas, and both killed members of the Gutierrez administration. In addition, other groups, including Carrancistas and conservatives, took advantage of this wave of violence to kidnap and kill their enemies while their propaganda machines continued blaming Villa and Zapata.

Ultimately, this wave of violence was the beginning of the end of the Convencionista alliance. Villa, Zapata, and President Gutierrez began showing signs of contempt and mistrust for each other. In addition, the president's inability to control his generals caused him enormous concern. If he could not even protect his own people from his generals, how could he expect to tell them how to use their armies to fight Carranza? Indeed, before the end of the month, President Gutierrez was already considering leaving the coalition.

THE COLLAPSE OF THE CONVENCIONISTA ALLIANCE

About a month after the triumphal Convencionista parade in Mexico City, the alliance fell apart. By late December 1914, President Eulalio Gutierrez began contacting members of the Convencionista forces who had no direct relation to Villa or Zapata, asking them to join him in an alternative coalition that he hoped would be reinforced with Carrancistas interested in avoiding a civil war. In particular, President Gutierrez made various unsuccessful attempts to convince General Obregon to join him and help him legitimize his government.

Villa heard rumors of President Gutierrez's intentions and went to confront the president. The president complained no reason existed for him to be president without any real authority over the Convencionista forces, and he explained that he was considering resigning. He criticized the wave of violence, particularly Berlanga's assassination and the threats against his minister Vasconcelos. Villa insensitively justified Berlanga's killing by saying that he "was a lap dog . . . always yapping at [Villa]."[4] President Gutierrez also complained that Villa, not Gutierrez or his administration, controlled the trains, telegraphs, and even the printing of money. These were important instruments of Villa's power and he refused to relinquish them. Villa considered arresting the president, but, having no hard evidence, simply told the president he could not resign. Gutierrez nodded but secretly continued trying to find a way to replace Villa.

Villa's Military Strategy Against Carranza

Even though the coalition was politically troubled, militarily it remained strong. As early as December 11, Villa sent one of his most important generals, Tomas Urbina, east to confront one of the strongest Carrancistas, General Pablo Gonzalez, in Tamaulipas. On December 15, Zapata confronted General Obregon and successfully took the city of Puebla, located between Mexico City and Carranza's stronghold at Veracruz. On December 17, General Natera took the western city of Guadalajara in the name of Villa.

Carranza's end appeared near. Nevertheless, General Angeles was concerned that Villa was not taking Carranza seriously and tried to convince Villa not to leave their victory to chance. Angeles explained the importance of giving Carranza a devastating blow at Veracruz with combined Villista and Zapatista forces. Had Villa followed Angeles's advice, it may have been the end of Carranza. However, Villa refused to listen to Angeles. Instead, he ordered him to head north to attack the city of Monterrey, the largest industrial city of the north, to open a second front against General Gonzalez. General Angeles could not understand the reasons behind Villa's refusal to go directly against Carranza and avoid a protracted war.

At the time, Angeles did not understand the regional aspect of Villa's power. Veracruz was out of his reach. Villa felt uncomfortable in Mexico City, too far from his homeland, and soon relocated further north in Zacatecas, closer to Chihuahua. Carranza had chosen the perfect place for his headquarters. Veracruz was not only a great port connecting his supporters in Mexico's northeast and southeast, but it was a safe haven that gave him enough room to regroup and reorganize his offensive against the Convencionistas.

Unlike the Constitucionalistas that recognized Carranza's leadership, Villa appeared more interested in getting rid of the president than in following his lead. On January 8, 1915, on his way to Monterrey, General Angeles found the evidence Villa needed to replace the president. At the city of Saltillo he captured Antonio Villarreal, one of the Carrancistas who received letters from President Gutierrez inviting him to form an independent coalition. After Angeles took the city, he found Villarreal's correspondence with the president. As soon as he learned about this, Villa sent a telegram asking one of his confidants in the capital, Jose Isabel Robles, to confront the president with the evidence. Villa ordered him to execute the president if he admitted having written such letters.

Robles, however, was conspiring with Gutierrez and planning to leave Villa. He warned the president and recommended he leave the capital. At 3:00 A.M. on January 15, President Gutierrez left Mexico City with Robles and several of his supporters, 10,000 troops, and 10 million pesos.[5] The president published a manifesto denouncing Villa and Zapata for the wave of violence and officially discharging them as leaders of the Convencionista army. He headed to his home state of San Luis Potosi where he expected to establish his government. However, General Urbina intercepted the convoy and confronted him. The president's troops were confused, since they considered themselves Villistas and did not know the reasons for the president's relocation or Urbina's threat. They refused to fight, so the president's entourage fled. Several of them found refuge in the United States. Gutierrez himself managed to escape to Carrancista territory, falling into oblivion.

The dissolution of the Convencionista government delegitimized Villa. For all practical purposes, Villa and Carranza, two rebels, now led a civil war. Only total military victory could legitimize either one. Nevertheless, Villa tried to retain his claim to legitimacy by naming Roque Gonzalez Garza president of Mexico, but it was obvious that he was simply Villa's puppet with no legitimacy from the convention. Furthermore, Mexico City was not a center of Villismo so the Gonzalez Garza government was established in the city of Queretaro. Politically, Mexico City had become an empty shell in Zapatista hands. Villa managed to provide some legitimacy to this government due to his charisma and the sheer strength of his army. After all, he was still considered, by most Mexicans and international observers including U.S. President Woodrow Wilson, to be the strongman in Mexico and the most likely victor of the civil war.

The Weakening of the Villa-Zapata Alliance

As President Gutierrez vanished, Villa's alliance with Zapata continued to deteriorate. Zapata's success at Puebla offered an excellent opportunity for Villa to join him and destroy Carranza. Instead, Villa busied himself with trying to destroy the Carrancista reductions in the north. In addition, Villa failed to send the promised weapons and ammunition so Zapata grew increasingly reluctant to collaborate with Villa. Villa's failure to send the weapons was not intentional. His economic policies in Chihuahua began to affect his ability to sustain his army, complicating his ability to make good his promise to Zapata. Tired of waiting for the promised weapons, Zapata, feeling vulnerable at the city of Puebla, decided to move his troops south to the town of Tlaltizapan. The most important opportunity to destroy Carranza was lost.

On January 25, Zapata withdrew even further south, resuming his local campaign in Morelos (his home state), and abandoned Mexico City. This action would be disastrous for Villa. Neither Zapata nor Villa understood the importance of the capital city. For all practical purposes Carranza's life had been spared and he could now claim the capital in the name of the Constitucionalistas. On January 28, General Obregon simply moved into Puebla and Mexico City without the need to fight. This also opened an important corridor by which Carranza could supply Obregon's forces as he moved north from Mexico City to confront Villa. As long as this corridor remained open, Obregon could count on the supplies he needed to fight Villa.

Villismo Takes the Offensive

As he was losing the center of the country, Villa remained the dominant force in the west and north regions. His reputation of invincibility was such that many times his victories were achieved by simply storming garrisons as his soldiers yelled, "¡*Viva Villa!*" Partly out of sheer terror and partly out of a desire to side with the victor, many Carrancistas readily surrendered. Villa appeared unstoppable.

Only the northeast continued resisting Villa's threat. Angeles took Monterrey and Urbina took San Luis Potosi, but the surrounded General Pablo Gonzalez continued resisting at Tamaulipas.

Benevolent Villismo

During his Monterrey campaign, General Angeles managed to add his own personal style to the faction of the Division of the North under his command. Contrary to Villa's famous massive cavalry charges, Angeles achieved his victories by minimizing bloodshed. At Saltillo, he tricked the Carrancistas by making them believe that the bulk of his forces were retreating west while leaving some 800 men dangerously exposed. The Constitucionalistas defending Saltillo took the bait and pursued these men, not realizing that they had left the city terribly exposed. Only 600 men defended the city. General Angeles sent General Emilio Madero, brother of the slain president, into Saltillo with 2,000 men, causing the immediate surrender of the city. Furthermore, Angeles refused to execute any of his prisoners. Thus, Angeles was reinforcing the image of "benevolent Villismo."

The Carrancistas who had abandoned Saltillo regrouped in the town of Ramos Arizpe in an effort to block Angeles's advance to Monterrey. However, General Angeles was right behind them and attacked before they could organize their defense. At that moment a dense fog enveloped the area—so dense that neither side could distinguish friend from foe. Both artilleries shot blindly, often killing their own troops. In spite of this complication, Angeles prevailed and captured Monterrey. Angeles offered amnesty to the 3,000 prisoners under one condition: the promise not to fight Villa ever again. Many joined Angeles's troops but some, especially officers, broke their promise as soon as they were freed, fleeing to Tampico to join General Gonzalez.

The rich city of Monterrey provided Villa with much needed wealth to support his army. With this in mind, General Angeles tried to attract the support of the upper class of Monterrey. He showed considerable respect to private property, refusing to confiscate any property, and also protected the church, an institution highly respected by this class. However, as soon as Villa took personal control of the city, he ordered the confiscation of property and forced taxes on the wealthy. Angeles believed Villa had destroyed the possibility of attracting key allies for his war effort and possible future government.

THE DECLINE OF THE DIVISION OF THE NORTH

After Monterrey, the city of Tampico was the most important strategic prize for Villa to gain control of the entire north of the country. However, Urbina, in charge of attacking that port city, proved less competent than Angeles and failed in his mission. Villa was furious; it was the first time during the civil war that Villista forces failed to take a major city. Some Carrancistas began to believe that it could be possible to stop Villa.

Urbina's failure was not the only strategic problem affecting Villa. Villa was spending too much energy trying to dominate the north, allowing Carranza to become increasingly strong in the center of the country. After Obregon's occupation of Mexico City, General Diegues re-occupied the city of Guadalajara. Once again, the Carrancistas did not need to fight. The Villistas had simply abandoned the city to join Villa in the north. The Carrancistas now controlled central Mexico from coast to coast, effectively dividing the Zapatistas in the south from the Villistas in the north. The long-term effect of this strategy was lethal for the Division of the North. From this moment on, Villa's forces began losing their military superiority against Carranza's forces.

General Obregon Takes the Lead

Villa finally realized that the expansion of Carrancistas had gone too far and decided to retake Guadalajara. However, in order to reach the city, he had to confront Obregon, who began moving north from Mexico City. As he approached his enemy, Villa had two major setbacks, but his overconfidence did not allow him to appreciate their importance and act more cautiously. First, General Angeles fell from his horse and his injuries prevented him from joining Villa for some time. Angeles

was one of Villa's most important strategic advisers and his expertise
in directing Villa's artillery had played a major role in his victories on
more than one occasion. However, Villa had become increasingly ar-
rogant and did not appreciate Angeles's contribution to his victories,
dismissing the importance of such a key general. Second, Villa's arms
providers in the United States were having serious problems buying
and shipping weapons and ammunition to him. In part the problem
was caused by World War I. Before that war began, Villa had enjoyed
practically full attention from weapon providers in the United States,
but now he had to compete with European buyers, and also with the
wealthier Carranza, all willing to pay higher prices. Villa believed he
had an easy solution to this problem: he would acquire weapons and
supplies by defeating Obregon. This solution became far more difficult
than Villa expected.

Villa was confident of an easy victory against Obregon. Affected by
his growing arrogance, he considered his opponent nothing more than a
simple obstacle on his way to Guadalajara. Not even low-rank Villistas
took this middle-class general seriously. They called him "the perfumed
one." They considered him too snobbish and refined to be a good war-
rior. Indeed, Obregon, a middle-class farmer turned general, was better
known for his political and diplomatic skills than his military deeds.
Nevertheless, he soon became Villa's most formidable opponent.

Overconfidence also caused Villa to overlook basic tactical concerns. First, Villa's General Urbina had been unable to take the oil-
rich port of Tampico and Zapata had not attempted to cut Obregon's
supply line. Second, Villa was giving Obregon too much room and time
to carefully position himself. All this allowed Obregon to move further
north without losing strength.

Contrary to Villa, Obregon behaved with extreme caution. He
moved north at a very slow pace, benefiting from the fact that nobody
was disturbing his march. This allowed him to avoid stretching too far
and too fast, and to avoid over-exposing his supply lines. This pace also
allowed him to carefully scout for and choose an adequate location for
the battle in which he could complicate Villa's well-known cavalry
charges. He found the ideal place outside the town of Celaya. The area
was crisscrossed with irrigation ditches that he could use as defensive
trenches. He planned to complement these obstructions with strategi-

cally located machine guns. Unlike Villa, Obregon did not underestimate his enemy's strength. His strategy was mainly defensive: contain Villa's attacks by exhausting the Villistas while trying to preserve his men's energy and ammunition for a counterattack. This strategy became the perfect formula against Villa's hitherto undefeatable Division of the North.

The First Battle of Celaya

Villa and Obregon clashed at Celaya on April 6, 1915. The initial confrontation occurred early in the morning and was provoked by one of Obregon's rare misjudgments. He thought Villa's forces were located further away in the nearby town of Irapuato. In reality Villa was much closer at the hacienda of El Guaje. Obregon sent his vanguard, commanded by General Fortunato Maycotte, to occupy the battlefield before Villa's arrival. Unexpectedly, Maycotte found himself facing Villa's army. The Villistas took advantage of the situation, reducing Maycotte's 1,500 soldiers to 500. Villa pursued the retreating Carrancistas, eventually facing Obregon's main army at the outskirts of Celaya. The Villistas pressed on, forcing the enemy to retreat behind their defenses. They fought the rest of the day, but Villa refrained from night attacks in order to save ammunition. He was sure that he could finish Obregon off the next morning.

At 5:00 A.M. sharp, Villa began bombarding Obregon's forces. Obregon's inferior artillery could not respond to the attack. As expected, Villa then sent his cavalry across the field, using wooden planks to facilitate the march through the ditches. However, Obregon's machine guns managed to contain the charge. Villa was determined to destroy Obregon. During the course of the day, Villa charged 40 times before finally breaking Obregon's defenses. Villa's victory appeared inevitable, but this time luck stood on Obregon's side. Overwhelmed by the attack, Obregon ordered his bugler to sound a retreat. This confused the Villistas, who believed the order was being given by their officers. Right at the moment when Villa's forces were ready to make the final blow, they retreated. By now, the Villistas were confused, disorganized, exhausted, and short of ammunition. Obregon did not miss this opportunity. He took the offensive, forcing the Division of the North to a humiliating retreat.

The First Battle of Celaya was very important for one particular reason: it destroyed Villa's image of invincibility. Obregon's soldiers began to believe that they could defeat Villa. Obregon's defensive strategy appeared to have worked, and his troops were eager to try it again. During this first battle, ammunition was a major concern for both camps. However, Obregon's strategy was more efficient while Villa's offensive wasted great quantities of ammunition and many lives. Aware of his short supplies, Villa suspended the night attacks, giving Obregon enough breathing space to reorganize his troops and to counterattack. Still, Villa believed that Obregon's victory had been pure luck, so he did not change his strategy.

The Second Battle of Celaya

Eager for a rematch, Villa partially solved the problem of the ammunition shortage. A shipment of weapons, intended for the first battle but delayed at the border at Ciudad Juarez, finally reached Villa. The shipment was not abundant, so once again he needed to ration his ammunition. Obregon also got additional supplies, but he too was forced to ration.

Villa realized that during the first battle the irrigation ditches had limited the effectiveness of his charges and exposed his cavalry to machine gun fire, so he tried to force Obregon to relocate for the next confrontation, citing alleged humanitarian concerns. On April 9, he sent a letter to Obregon requesting they move away from the city of Celaya in order to avoid civilian casualties. To add pressure, he also sent copies of this letter to the U.S., French, German, and British consuls at Celaya. These diplomats agreed with Villa and pressured Obregon to move away from the city. Obregon, who had proven that this location favored his strategy, refused. Instead, he strengthened his position by installing barbed wire—to further complicate Villa's advancement over the ditches—and increasing the number of machine guns. Both sides received additional troops, but Obregon now had an advantage. He had 18,000 soldiers against Villa's 15,000 troops.

Aware of all this, Villa decided to attack as soon as possible and cut short Obregon's defensive preparations. At six in the morning on April 13, Villa began to mobilize his troops. On this occasion, Obregon distributed his forces over a wider territory, creating a very long line of defense. Villa had two options: he could concentrate his attack on one point in order to penetrate and surround the defenses from behind, or he could spread his forces out and attack all the defenses simultaneously. Convinced of his capacity to overwhelm Obregon, he decided for the latter option. His artillery was not as effective precisely because Obregon's spread alignment did not offer big targets. The brunt of the attack would fall on Villa's cavalry as it opened the field for his infantry. The ditches and the additional barbed wire and machine guns complicated this operation, leading to enormous casualties. Nevertheless, the Villistas managed to sustain their massive attack for most of the day and were about to break the defenses when, once again, nightfall forced Villa to recall his troops.

Villa was determined not to allow Obregon to reorganize his defenses, so at midnight he cautiously moved his troops forward in order to surprise Obregon at daybreak. However, Obregon was able to contain Villa once more. Villa's attack failed because of the quality of the ammunition he had received via Ciudad Juarez. Soldiers began to complain that they were shooting "wooden bullets." It appears that the last shipment contained a considerable amount of cartridges holding only a quarter of the gunpowder needed, so the bullets failed to reach beyond 50 yards.[6] Still, during the day, the Villistas came close several times to breaking the defenses but, once again, darkness forced them to stop the fight.

On April 15, Villa tried one last time to break Obregon's defenses with a massive attack at daybreak. He was determined to succeed, so he personally led his forces in the battlefield. Two of his horses were reportedly killed during the battle, but both times he jumped on a new horse and continued fighting. However, after another full day of fighting, both sides were exhausted and running out of ammunition without a clear advantage on either side.

Concerned with the lack of ammunition, Obregon decided to take the offensive. He had kept 6,000 cavalry units in reserve. Villa had used all his forces and had no reserves. His exhausted troops were no match for Obregon's fresh ones. Obregon's attack was timely and chaos ensued among the exhausted Villistas. They broke formation and ran to their trains. Most of the trains got away. Only injured soldiers were captured as their train did not manage to leave on time.

For the second time, Obregon appeared to have won the day. This time Obregon's victory was clear. Villa was forced to retreat, suffering a higher number of casualties. Obregon reportedly lost 1,000 men to Villa's 3,000, and an additional 6,000 Villistas were captured. The general in charge of the prisoners, General Benjamin Hill, promised clemency and asked all captured officers to step forward. About 120 men did. General Hill promptly sent them to the firing squad.

The Battle of Leon

The Second Battle of Celaya was the most devastating defeat of Villa's career. The Division of the North was left considerably weakened and incapable of attempting a rematch. Villa had to retreat, regrouping his army further north near the city of Leon.

Obregon decided to err on the side of caution and did not pursue Villa immediately. Instead, he continued carefully moving north while making sure that his line of supplies remained safe. For the next two months there was no confrontation. Both sides simply observed each other's movements, looking for the enemy to make a strategic mistake that could give them an advantage, but to no avail.

By now, Angeles's injury had healed enough to allow him to join Villa. He recommended Villa move further north to Torreon, where they could strengthen their troops and supplies while Obregon would be forced to stretch his own line too thin. Villa, convinced that Obregon's victories had been a matter of luck, did not listen to Angeles's advice. He did not want to appear wounded and defeated, so he decided to hold his ground, determined to confront Obregon at Leon.

Villa could have gained a considerable advantage if he had focused on interrupting Obregon's supplies. To Villa's dismay, Tomas Urbina continued to fail at taking the wealthy city of Tampico while Zapata, aware of the possibility of a Carranza victory, finally made an effort to disrupt Obregon's lines. This mission required sending peasant militias to enemy territory without the protection and resources of friendly villagers. Aware of this vulnerability, Zapata had only made a haphazard attack on Obregon's trains and soon retreated to friendly territory.

Ammunition continued to be an issue. Villa's own supplies were seriously affected by his double defeat at Celaya. His agent in the United

States, Felix Sommerfeld, became worried that he might end up on the losing side, so he decided to offer the weapons to Carranza instead. Villa was unable to find new suppliers. Sommerfeld then decided not to sell his weapons to Carranza either, but to the Germans making preparations for a possible conflict in Europe on the eve of World War I. In the end, both Villa and Obregon continued rationing their ammunition as they prepared for their third confrontation.

Throughout May, Villa and Obregon engaged each other in small skirmishes with no major results. Obregon knew that a big part of his winning strategy had been forcing Villa to engage in an all-out attack while Obregon held his ground, conserving bullets and his men's energy. Obregon doubted that Villa was capable of taking the offensive. Concerned that these endless skirmishes would exhaust his meager supplies, Obregon decided to take the offensive.

Obregon ordered his officers to prepare an offensive for June 5. Fortunately for him, Villa was also desperate and had made a similar decision for an earlier date. Obregon's successes had depended on his defensive strategy of containment and counterattack. Villa's impulsive nature allowed him to try it again. On the night of May 30, Villa ordered his cavalry to take a very cumbersome path to surround an unsuspecting Obregon. The following morning, they attacked Obregon's camp from the rear. The surprise attack forced Obregon to retreat while the Villistas captured a train wagon full of ammunition.

Villa's surprise attack against Obregon's forces had succeeded, so Villa decided to press on. On June 3, he ordered a massive bombardment in preparation for his next offensive. Obregon met with his generals at a hacienda, Santa Ana, to assess the situation. As he was crossing the patio of the hacienda, an artillery shell exploded by his side. A startled Obregon realized that his right arm had been blown away. Believing that he was bleeding to death, he grabbed his pistol, put it on his temple, and pulled the trigger. Fortunately for him, and for Carranza, the night before his assistant had cleaned the gun and forgot to put the bullets back in. Obregon was taken to a hospital in the nearby town of Trinidad. Unaware of the situation, Villa was unable to take advantage of this vacuum of leadership and did not press the attack right away. Instead, he limited that day's assault to artillery bombardment.

The next day, Obregon's generals promptly reorganized the line of command and launched an attack, taking Villa by surprise. Unlike Villa, they concentrated all their cavalry and infantry attacks on a single spot in Villa's defenses. The reinforcements that could have contained this attack were absent. This was the cavalry that had attacked Obregon's camp from the rear. The Villista defense broke apart and Villa struggled to maintain his forces. He retreated in stages, trying to regroup and repel the attack, but Obregon's forces continued the pressure, forcing Villa to order a full retreat. Villa had suffered his third major defeat in a row. He loaded his trains and relocated further north to Aguascalientes. The Battle of Leon would later be considered the final blow that broke the mighty Division of the North. Villa, however, was not ready to give up.

The Battle of Aguascalientes

As Villa reached Aguascalientes, his agents in the United States finally sent him several trains loaded with weapons and ammunition. Was it too late? Villa's army was demoralized and dangerously weakened. However, the shipment raised morale in the midst of defeat. Villa hoped for a master stroke that could bring him back to his previous superior strength. Villa decided not to rely on Zapata anymore and sent his own men to cut Obregon's supply line. He met with two of his most reliable officers, Rodolfo Fierro and Canuto Reyes, and ordered them to march south with 3,000 cavalrymen. The task was not an easy one. They had to infiltrate enemy territory under a stronger Obregon and a weaker Villa. They successfully took side roads, avoiding detection. They encountered some manageable resistance and retook the small garrison that Obregon had left protecting Leon. They managed to destroy the train tracks, successfully disrupting Obregon's supply lines. Emboldened, Fierro and Reyes took an audacious step and continued south, where they briefly occupied Mexico City.

Regardless of these minor victories, Villa's window for a comeback was rapidly vanishing. The morale of his troops was at its lowest level. Many were convinced that Obregon had won the civil war, and they began abandoning Villa. Even the mayor of Ciudad Juarez tried to negotiate the surrender of the city to Carranza, but his intentions were discovered in time for Villa to replace him. Fearing Villa's retaliation, the mayor escaped to El Paso. A more serious desertion was that of one of his top generals, General Tomas Urbina. After his failure at Tamaulipas, Urbina was demoralized and refused to join Villa at Aguascalientes. He claimed to suffer from health problems and told Villa that he was retiring with his escort to his hacienda, Las Nieves. Villa would never forgive him. Another important general who not present at Aguascalientes was General Angeles, but this was for a very different reason. Villa sent him to the United States on a diplomatic mission to try to regain President Wilson's support. Angeles would fail in his assignment. After Villa's defeats, the U.S. president became more interested in supporting Carranza.

Luck appeared to have abandoned Villa. He was now weaker than Obregon. Even the successful mission carried out by Fierro and Reyes disappointed him. They had cut Obregon's lines, but after a train loaded with guns and supplies had already passed Leon. Villa's upcoming confrontation against Obregon at Aguascalientes was the first one without either side suffering a scarcity of supplies, but Obregon fared better in almost all other aspects. The wounds from his amputated arm healed fairly quickly and well enough for him to command his army. And, even though both increased their number of soldiers, Obregon's troops still outnumbered Villa's 14,000 men by 3,000. Villa had recalled the troops abandoned by General Urbina, but there were simply not enough men. Nevertheless, news of a possible military buildup alarmed Obregon, so he decided to attack as soon as possible.

On July 6, Obregon began his march to Aguascalientes. Villa initially decided to act cautiously and wait for Obregon, but patience was not in his nature. Once again, he changed his mind, surprising Obregon with an offensive on July 8. Villa surrounded Obregon, attacking on all fronts, but Obregon managed to hold his defenses. The intensity of the battles was such that, by the second day, Obregon was already running out of ammunition. Having no alternative, Obregon decided to risk everything on an all-out assault the next day.

The next morning, Obregon responded by attacking the Villista trenches on two fronts. The Villistas' low morale had devastating consequences. They believed that Obregon's forces had surrounded them, and they panicked. Villa sent two supportive brigades, but they failed to arrive before the defenders had abandoned their positions. Villa was de-feated and forced to retreat for a fourth consecutive time. All was lost.

Time and time again Obregon had managed to defeat Villa. The once mighty Division of the North was now a defeated army in shatters. Villa was still in charge of 2,000 soldiers, but he was too weak to engage Obregon in formal battle. He disbanded his army into small units and laid low for some time to recover, waiting for the right opportunity to re-emerge. He took a few hundred men with him and retreated all the way back to Chihuahua. During this march he hid his remaining weapons, ammunition, and money in the hopes of a future opportunity.

Difficult Time for Villa in Chihuahua

When he returned in mid-July, Villa found Chihuahua completely changed. A great number of Chihuahuans, believing that Carranza had won the civil war, were less inclined to support Villa. But, per-haps even more discouraging, Chihuahua's finances were collapsing. A major problem was that most of the cattle stock had been depleted after several years of war and confiscations. In addition, Villa's defeats depreciated his currency and soon it became worthless. Businessmen and merchants on both sides of the border had been willing to accept Villa's currency because they expected him to eventually rule the coun-try, but now everybody was trying to get rid of this money and would only accept silver or gold. As revenue declined, the state fell into an inflationary spiral, further affecting Villa's deteriorating finances and popularity.

Angry, Villa blamed "greedy merchants" for his financial misfortune and tried to intimidate them into keeping prices down. He imprisoned them and kept them without food for two days, so as to make them experience the suffering endured by poor people.[7] This action did not help his cause. Fear and insecurity convinced many wealthy Chihua-huans that they had no alternative but to flee, abandoning their busi-nesses. Desperate, Villa began taxing the hitherto untouched wealth of U.S. merchants, hacendados, and miners. However, many Americans had refused to reactivate their businesses before the end of hostilities, so there were not enough of them to tax, offering a limited solution to his economic difficulties.

VILLA ATTEMPTS TO REBUILD HIS ARMY

In August, Villa began planning his comeback. He tried to find new means of supporting his troops. He visited villages and forced all their healthy men to choose between joining him or standing before the firing squad. Villa confiscated the possessions of those who managed to leave town and hide before he arrived. Whenever he found former Villistas, he showed no mercy. On one occasion, Villa lured some Carrancistas toward the hacienda of Santa Ana. He prepared an ambush and captured 187 prisoners. He incorporated 100 of them into his army. The remaining 87 had been Villistas, so he simply had them all shot.[8]

Realizing that he had exhausted Chihuahua's wealth, Villa looked to other regions that were economically stable, such as the neighboring state of Sonora. This state had experienced limited warfare during the revolution so its economy was fairly stable. Furthermore, Governor Jose Maria Maytorena had been his ally and was a well-known anti-Carrancista. Carranza only had a small garrison of 3,000 soldiers located in the border town of Agua Prieta under General Plutarco E. Calles. Villa hoped that he could easily defeat them and use this victory to rebuild his army. He hoped he could then move his army south, following the Pacific coast and joining Zapata's army. Villa expected that together they could retake Mexico City and resume their position of power. The plan was extremely optimistic, but technically not impossible. It was certainly not the first time that Villa attempted to build an army out of nothing. Huerta, for example, never imagined that Villa and his six men crossing the Rio Grande could become the formidable army that defeated him. However, the new situation was quite different. There were far more people willing to side with a victorious Carranza than with the president's murderer. It was also not clear how he expected this alliance to work now, since it had failed when he was the most powerful man in Mexico. Nevertheless, he was determined to rise again from the ashes.

Abandoning Villa

Villa's plan encountered serious problems from the very beginning. Perhaps the most damaging problem occurred on October 15, 1915. That day President Wilson officially recognized Carranza as the legitimate leader of the revolution.[9] Adding injury to this insult, many of

Villa's most important generals believed everything was lost and began abandoning him. General Raul Madero, for instance, believed that Villa had become a liability for the Convencionistas and asked him to step down as the head of its armed forces. Villa ignored him, so Raul resigned instead. In early September, General Angeles was on his way back from his unsuccessful diplomatic mission to the United States when he received the bad news about the Battle of Aguascalientes. He considered this the final blow to Villismo and decided not to return to Mexico. He bought a small ranch, establishing his residence near El Paso, Texas. General Panfilo Natera, who had remained governor of Zacatecas, joined Carranza, delivering the city to Villa's enemy. Even Governor Maytorena, when he heard of Villa's plan, feared that Sonora would become the next battleground, so he decided to flee. This opened the door for Obregon's forces, who easily occupied Hermosillo, taking official control over the entire state.

Villa's Revenge Against Deserters

Villa was outraged and considered all desertions personal betrayals. He became paranoid and vengeful. Perhaps the most dramatic example of Villa's wrath was what happened to General Urbina. Villa knew that Urbina's main reason for joining the revolution was personal enrichment and he was convinced that Urbina failed to take Tampico because he had been bribed. In addition, Villa was angry because Urbina refused to join him at the decisive battle at Aguascalientes. He placed this defeat squarely on Urbina's shoulders and decided that it was time to make an example out of him. One night in early September, Villa and a group of men stormed Urbina's hacienda, Las Nieves. In the resulting shootout Urbina was injured in one arm. As soon as he realized that Villa was among the attackers, he ordered his men to hold fire. Urbina invited Villa to his house and they had a long conversation. Urbina believed he had convinced Villa that he was still loyal to him and they appeared on good terms again. Urbina left his hacienda to seek medical attention. On his way to a nearby town, Fierro, who had stormed Las Nieves with Villa, caught up with Urbina's car and forced him out. Urbina was immediately executed and his body buried on the side of the road. Villa had sent a clear message to his former supporters.

Carranza and U.S. troops use trains in search for Villa—Mexican-U.S. campaign after Villa, 1916. (Library of Congress.)

As far as he was concerned, desertion was an act of treason punishable by death. Villa began hunting down former Villistas.

After Urbina's murder, Villa searched Las Nieves trying to find the gold and silver that Urbina had accumulated during years of plundering haciendas and towns. Unable to find anything, Villa left Officer Ramirez with a few men to continue searching. Villa told him that they could keep 1/3 of the money found. Eventually they found 50 bars of gold. Fearing that Villa could kill them in order to keep the whole treasure, Ramirez decided to join the Carrancistas. Not surprisingly, the Carrancista officers confiscated all the gold.[10]

The Crossing into Sonora

Despite all his difficulties, Villa gathered 6,000 men, kept his spirits high, and went ahead with his plan to go to Sonora. He did not seem to notice that his army was only a shadow of the once mighty Division of the North. Their morale, ammunition, and food were all in short supply. However, those who remained with him were hardcore Villistas and kept the faith that their leader could lead them to a new comeback. Villa considered this journey a safe one because few train tracks connected Sonora with the rest of Mexico, complicating the possibility of Carranza reinforcing Agua Prieta's garrison.

On October 6, Villa and his men began crossing the rough high peaks of the Sierra Madre mountain range dividing Sonora and Chihuahua. The ensuing march through the desert was dreadful. During this journey, they endured snow storms, scorching heat, thirst, and hunger. There was a particularly difficult crossing at El Pulpito Canyon. The climb was so steep that Villa was forced to leave his artillery behind. The limited food and water convinced many of his soldiers that this plan was suicidal and they left him. It was at this desperate time that Villa lost one of his most important and loyal associates, Rodolfo Fierro. Deaf to anybody's advice, Fierro forced his horse to cross a deep swamp. The horse was unable to swim and flipped over. Fierro got caught at the bottom and drowned.

The Battle at Agua Prieta

Villa's excursion appeared destined to fail, but not everything was bad news for him. General Francisco Urbalejo, commanding a small force of Yaqui Indians, easily occupied the town of Naco overlooking his target: Agua Prieta. After almost a full month of hardship Villa was finally in front of 7,500 troops ready to storm Agua Prieta. Villa's troops practically doubled the number of defenders, but General Calles had been expecting him and was well prepared. Mimicking the success at Celaya, he mined the field, installed barbed wired, and positioned 18 machine guns to defend the garrison. Unknown to Villa, in addition to his 3,000 men, Calles was about to receive an additional 6,000 troops that Carranza had managed to send to Calles via U.S. territory. Villa did not foresee that President Wilson, now recognizing Carranza, would allow the transportation of Mexican soldiers from Texas to Arizona and into Agua Prieta. President Wilson was concerned about developments in Europe and seemed anxious to solve the conflict in Mexico as soon as possible.

Villa only found out about the arrival of enemy reinforcements after the fight had started. He was confused and enraged. His offensive was no match for the reinforced defenses. Villa tried to regain some kind of advantage by fighting at night, but, as he began to mobilize his troops, searchlights illuminated the battlefield, exposing the Villistas to Calles's fire. Electricity for these lights as well as additional electrification for the barbed wire was also provided by the United States. Villa had no alternative but to retreat, swearing revenge against all Americans.

The Naco Manifesto

Villa relocated his troops back to Naco. There, on November 9, 1915, he made public a manifesto accusing both presidents, Wilson and Carranza, of having a secret deal. Villa had no real evidence for this, but he based his accusations on previous proposals that U.S. officials had made to him. He simply assumed that the same deal had been offered to Carranza. According to the *Naco Manifesto*, Carranza was leasing Magdalena Bay for a U.S. military base in the Mexican Pacific and the Tehuantepec Strait for the transportation of U.S. army personnel and supplies from the Gulf of Mexico to the Pacific Ocean. Villa insisted that this secret deal forced the Mexican government to make political and economic concessions that benefited the United States, but would result in the loss of jobs and economic opportunities for Mexicans.

This manifesto redefined Villa's reason to fight. Anti-American rhetoric was his new attempt to legitimize his struggle. From this moment forward, he considered foreigners, particularly U.S. citizens, his primary enemies. His fight, he insisted, was to save Mexican sovereignty.

The Emergence of a More Sinister Villa

In the aftermath of the Sonora campaign Villa was transformed. Not only was his reason to fight different, but now he had no reliable source of revenue and became even more enraged about betrayals, including the very people that he had hitherto protected. Thus, his famous Robin Hood-like attitude was replaced by a more sinister approach. He began a murderous campaign against Americans as well as villagers and peons he thought had turned against him. He began executing anybody who refused to support him or who resisted his demands for supplies and volunteers. Carranza used Villa's new attitude to strengthen his propaganda reassuring Mexicans that Villa had never ceased to be anything more than a bloodthirsty bandit.

One of Villa's most infamous attacks against civilians took place during his journey from Sonora back into Chihuahua. By now many towns throughout Mexico had created their own *defensas sociales*, a sort of community militia, to protect their property and people from the abuses committed during the revolution. In early December, a group of Villistas approached San Pedro de las Cuevas. The villagers did not recognize them so they ambushed them, killing a few. Realizing their mistake they stopped shooting and explained their error to the leader, Macario Bracamonte. Bracamonte understood and decided not to punish the town. However, Villa was furious when he arrived at Las Cuevas and learned about the ambush. He ordered the immediate apprehension of all adult men from the town. The next day about 70 of them were executed.

The Official End of the Division of the North

Upon his return to Ciudad Chihuahua, Villa officially dissolved what was left of his shattered Division of the North. He had no other alternative. He had less than 2,000 men and had lost the financial means to arm, feed, and dress them. Without his army he also lost control of the state. On December 23, 1915, the Carrancista general, Jacinto Treviño, occupied the abandoned capital of the state and became its governor. Most of Villa's remaining generals refused to continue fighting and tried to convince Villa to negotiate an amnesty, but he was not ready to completely give up. Instead, he convinced a few officers to stay with him, hoping that Carranza's selling out to the Americans would soon help him create a strong anti-Carrancista alliance. For now, however, he had no option but to hide and wait. He met with his remaining officers at the hacienda of Bustillos, told them his plan, and ordered them to split the army into small guerilla forces. There was a double benefit in doing that. The Carrancistas would find it more difficult to track and capture these small groups and, at the same time, each one of them could find their own means of supplying their forces through sneak attacks on small garrisons or by forcing villagers and merchants to pay "security taxes." For all practical purposes, Villa become a bandit once again.

Exiled in the United States?

Like most Mexicans, President Wilson expected Villa to surrender soon. To expedite this he offered him political asylum in the United States. This would, he hoped, guarantee a peaceful end to the revolution and, since Villa's well-being was guaranteed, avoid the threat of Villa's resurgence. When news of this amnesty became public, some people in the United States were eager to make money off of such a famous guest. Most notably, Courtney Riley Cooper visited El Paso in order to explore the possibility of creating a "Pancho Villa Show" to tour the country. He had in mind a repeat of the famous "Buffalo Bill's Wild West Show."

Sadly for Mr. Cooper, Villa refused the U.S. president's offer. The president was puzzled; he did not understand Villa. But while it was common for political leaders to go into exile after a serious defeat in a civil war or *coup d'etat*, Villa was not a stereotypical leader. He belonged to his homeland. For Villa there was no alternative but to live in Chihuahua or Durango. Anywhere else he would be an alien without a soul. Everything he knew and everything he cared for was in Chihuahua. Even after all his defeats and his current violent attitude toward the population, he still believed he was the only person in Mexico who could bring justice and prosperity to the poor people of Chihuahua. Still, he was prepared to die fighting in Chihuahua instead of leaving to live peacefully in exile.

Reason to Continue Fighting

By early 1917, Villa had developed the attitude of a desperate man on the run with no real reason to fight but no obvious exit strategy, either. Instead of seeking a truce agreement, he continued fighting, but he was a defeated general and his capacity to cause harm was considerably reduced. A number of Villistas joined Carranza as a protection from Villa's wrath and even those who remained by his side were not clear about why Villa continued fighting. Villa did little to explain himself, causing low morale, confusion, and disappointment among those who still remained with him. By now, practically everybody believed that the capture of Villa was only a matter of time.

Villa tried to continue relying on the *Naco Manifesto* to justify his struggle. He added that he was protecting Mexico from Carranza's plan to sell its northern territories to President Wilson. He was trying to force desertion among Carrancistas, but he never provided any convincing evidence. No matter what his nationalist rhetoric said, his real reason to continue fighting was clearly his obsession with destroying Carranza.

Villa continued believing in his capacity to recreate his mighty Division of the North. In addition to Carrancista deserters, he hoped to attract large number of volunteers once again. This hope received a boost when Chihuahuans showed outrage against the new Carrancista governor, General Treviño, who ruled Chihuahua as an occupied territory. Instead of allowing local and state elections, he appointed military outsiders to both government and military positions. These officials used their position of power for personal enrichment with little interest in helping the suffering Chihuahuans. Extortion and corruption by these authorities was so obvious that many Chihuahuans began remembering Villa's government nostalgically. But most Chihuahuans were tired of the endless fighting, so he was unable to attract nearly as many volunteers as he had hoped.

Carranza's Economic Plan for Chihuahua

In reaction to Governor Treviño's negative influence, Carranza and Obregon began considering a different strategy to destroy Villa. After six years of continued fighting, the state needed a program for economic recovery. Carranza had no intention of continuing Villa's populist policies of land and social reform. His first priority was pacification. Like Porfirio Diaz before him, he hoped that peace would attract investors and entrepreneurs back to the state. He expected that the resulting economic recovery and prosperity would eliminate, or at least reduce, popular unrest and any lingering support for Villa. With this in mind, he asked Obregon to meet on January 8, 1916, with U.S. businessmen and financiers to encourage investment in the state.[11] Obregon assured them that Villa had ceased to be a threat in the region and encouraged them to invest in their haciendas and mines to reactivate agricultural and industrial production. Obregon had gained enormous respect for his victories against Villa, but financiers, hacendados, miners, and merchants were not sure that he was able to protect them as long as Villa remained on the loose.

This was a lesson for Carranza and Obregon. Villa was obviously defeated, but, as long as he continued roaming Chihuahua's countryside, the government could not begin any real policies to consolidate the state. The last phase of Villa's revolutionary career consisted of an effort by Carrancista authorities in Chihuahua to eliminate Villa, one way or another, and thus effectively end the emergence of another military phase of the revolution and begin the construction of a revolutionary state.

NOTES

1. Friedrich Katz, *The Life and Times of Pancho Villa* (Stanford, CA: Stanford University Press, 1998), 436.

2. Ibid., 456.

3. Frank McLynn, *Villa and Zapata: A History of the Mexican Revolution* (New York: Carroll and Graf Publishers, 2000), 281.

4. Katz, *Life and Times of Pancho Villa*, 461.

5. Paco Ignacio Taibo II, *Pancho Villa: Una biografía narrativa* (Mexico: Editorial Planeta, 2006), 480.

6. Ibid., 518.

7. Katz, *Life and Times of Pancho Villa*, 512.

8. Taibo, *Pancho Villa*, 605.

9. Robert L. Scheina, *Villa: Soldier of the Mexican Revolution* (Washington, DC: Potomac Books, 2004), 73.

10. Katz, *Life and Times of Pancho Villa*, 523.

11. Taibo, *Pancho Villa*, 601.

Chapter 6

A NOT SO PEACEFUL
END (1916–1923)

Pancho Villa became a runaway impossible to capture. Not only Carranza, but also the U.S. government, risked wasting considerable resources and damaging their reputations while failing to capture the elusive Villa. In the meantime, Villa began a campaign to link Carranza's administration to the U.S. military expedition that entered Mexico to capture him. His plan was to cause outrage among Carrancista nationalists and convince them to help him fight Carranza and his American friends. However, his attempt to build an anti-Carrancista alliance was as elusive to Villa as he was to Carranza and the Americans. Villa spent the last phase of the Mexican Revolution on the run without any real political goal. Villa's reason for fighting was limited to refusing to accept Carranza's victory. In the end, Villa resembled more the bloodthirsty bandit of Carranza's propaganda than the heroic revolutionary he claimed to be. Once he realized that fact, he sought amnesty so he could rejoin civilian life. This last phase of the revolution was characterized by merciless brutality, although, due to the diminished Villista force, the death toll was smaller than that suffered during previous phases.

VILLA'S ANTI-AMERICAN CAMPAIGN

After Villa's defeat, Carranza tried to consolidate his power in Chihuahua, but he soon found out that it would be impossible while Villa roamed the land. As part of Carranza's efforts to win the hearts and minds of Chihuahuans, Obregon organized a conference to convince U.S. businessmen and investors that Chihuahua was safe for business. Two days later, Villa proved Obregon wrong. One of Villa's lieutenants, Pablo Lopez, attacked a passenger train near the town of Santa Isabel. On it were 20 U.S. employees of the Cusihuirachic Mine Company. Lopez ordered their capture. Villa's men found 19 of them. The Americans were forced out of the train, ordered to strip naked, and executed. The Villistas proceeded to rob the rest of the passengers, but Lopez ordered them to stop. Obviously influenced by Villa's *Naco Manifesto*, he explained that their enemies were the Americans and that all Mexicans must stand together against the enemy trying to appropriate northern Mexico. No one ever proved that Villa had explicitly ordered this massacre, but it succeeded at scaring Americans from reactivating their economic activities in Chihuahua. In the long run, however, this attack had a more negative effect on Villa's reputation than on Carranza's power. Due to his new policy of targeting U.S. citizens, he lost most of the supporters he had in the United States.

A week after the Santa Isabel massacre, Villa attempted his first attack on U.S. territory. He ordered a few hundred men to march with him to the border town of Ojinaga; no explanations were given. In route, he haphazardly explained his intention to attack the U.S. town across the border. Fearing the wrath of the U.S. army, many of his men deserted the mission. A handful remained with him, but they were not enough, so Villa was forced to suspend the attack.

THE ATTACK ON COLUMBUS, NEW MEXICO

After securing enough men, mainly through forced conscription, Villa was ready to try once more an attack on U.S. territory. This time, he clearly explained to his men the importance of this mission. He insisted that Carranza and the U.S. government had established an agreement under which Carranza would sell northern Mexico to the Americans. As proof, he mentioned the U.S. support that allowed Carranza's victory at Agua Prieta. He added that he was interested in targeting Samuel Ravel, a resident of Columbus, New Mexico and an arms trader who refused to deliver some of the weapons Villa had so desperately needed at the battles of Celaya. Ravel owned two hotels and two stores in Columbus that Villa intended to destroy as an act of revenge. In order to secure the support of his soldiers, Villa also reminded them of an incident in El Paso during which U.S. jailers had accidentally burned 20 Mexican prisoners alive while trying to delouse them with a mix that contained kerosene. In his speech, Villa mentioned this incident, appealing to anti-American sentiments and the need for revenge.

The Strategy

It is not completely clear what Villa's strategic reason was for attacking U.S. territory. Obviously, revenge and his new anti-Americanism were important reasons for Villa's action, but it is possible that he had a more practical reason. Villa knew perfectly well that the U.S. government would not let any attack against U.S. civilians go unpunished, much less if it occurred on U.S. soil. It seems likely that Villa was trying to force a U.S. intervention in Mexico. He could benefit from this in two ways: Carranza would be forced to condemn the intervention, as he had done in Veracruz. If this happened, Villa hoped, Mexico would be united against the invaders, and Villa could re-emerge as the leader of the Chihuahuan forces. If Carranza refused to condemn the intervention, Villa could claim that, indeed, there was a secret pact between the U.S. and Mexican presidents. He hoped that this could convince many Carrancistas to join him against the invaders and Carranza.

Ravel's town, Columbus, New Mexico, was a very small town of a few hundred people and a small garrison. Militarily and economically it presented an easy target of little importance, but it might well produce the same reaction from the U.S. government as would an attack on a larger target.

As Villa advanced toward the border, he made sure to remain as invisible as possible. He moved his troops only at night and captured anyone found in their path who could expose them. At some point he captured three Americans. He killed the two men, but spared the life of a woman. Regardless of all these precautions, U.S. officers received intelligence of Villa's approach. They did not know the reason, but they certainly did not expect an attack. There were rumors that Villa was making his way into the United States to smooth his relationship with President Woodrow Wilson and explain that he had had nothing to do with the Santa Isabel massacre. In any event, no defensive measures were taken.

As Villa approached Columbus, he sent scouts ahead to assess the target. They gathered very inaccurate data of Camp Furlong, the town's military garrison. They believed that it contained 50 soldiers while in reality there were close to 600. They also made a sketch of the garrison's layout, but in it they confused the barracks with the stable.

The Attack

On March 9, 1916, at 4:45 A.M., Villa attacked Columbus, New Mexico. He divided his 500 men into two detachments, one to storm Camp Furlong and the other to storm the town, rob the bank, and kill Sam Ravel. He remained across the border with a small escort. Camp Furlong was taken completely by surprise. Most of the officers were sleeping at their homes across town so they were unable to coordinate their men. However, very soon everything turned against the Villistas. Because the Villistas mistakenly targeted the stable and not the barracks, the sleeping U.S. soldiers had enough time to recover from the surprise and used machine guns to respond to the attack. The Villistas did not expect that many well-armed soldiers, so they were forced to retreat.

Meanwhile, things were not any better in town. The Villistas failed to find Mr. Ravel and were unable to open the bolt of the bank. During the shootout, they killed four guests at Ravel's Commercial Hotel. Suddenly, armed civilians began shooting at them from many different directions while the soldiers from Camp Furlong joined the counteroffensive. The defenders found it difficult to target the Villistas because of the lack of street lights, but at that point the Villistas made a vital mistake. After failing to find Ravel, they set fire to one of his hotels, lighting up the town. U.S. soldiers and civilians then were able to shoot at them, forcing them to retreat.

In the aftermath, none of Villa's immediate goals were achieved. He lost more than 100 men to Columbus's 17, most of them civilians. This fiasco, however, helped Villa to achieve his main goal: the U.S. government began preparations to invade Mexico.

The Consequence of the Attack

The next day, without consulting the president of Mexico, President Wilson announced that he was sending troops to Mexico to capture Pancho Villa. President Carranza found himself in a difficult position. Allowing the expedition to enter Mexico was an attack on Mexican sovereignty. Carranza had built his reputation on his unconditional nationalism, so he had the obligation to condemn the invasion. However, sending troops to stop the expedition could escalate the situation into a possible war with the United States, a war he could ill afford. However, allowing U.S. soldiers to hunt down Villa would facilitate his attempt to consolidate power and pacify Mexico. He decided to carefully navigate between these two options. He publicly condemned the presence of U.S. soldiers in Mexican territory on more than one occasion, but offered no resistance. In fact, whenever necessary he offered discreet assistance to the U.S. expedition.

It only took a couple of days for General John J. Pershing to gather 5,000 men to form the expedition. The Pershing Punitive Expedition, as this incursion became known, entered Mexico on March 15, 1916. Military planners proposed to President Wilson a major "campaign of pacification" of northern Mexico that included sending 250,000 troops and blocking all major Mexican ports.[1] However, politics soon limited the scope of the expedition. President Wilson, already concerned with the possibility of U.S. participation in World War I, rejected any action that could destabilize the Mexican government. He ordered the expedition limited to the capture of Villa. U.S. military commanders, puzzled by the idea of waging war against a single man who could hide anywhere, even outside of Mexico, suggested instead as their mission the destruction of Villismo. The president assented.

The Resurgence of Villa

Far from destroying Villa, the Punitive Expedition offered him a new life. Villa's claim that Carranza was selling the north to the United States became more believable when thousands of U.S. troops roamed the Chihuahuan countryside. Surprisingly, there was little recrimination against Villa for having provoked the invasion in the first place. Most villagers did not like having U.S. soldiers roaming their land and deliberately provided misleading intelligence to them. Carrancista generals also refused to provide assistance or information to General Pershing. Some refused to continue the campaign against Villa as long as U.S. troops remained in Mexico.

Villa tried to take advantage of this and convince these generals to turn against Carranza. Indeed, many of them were upset, and even frustrated, with Carranza's refusal to stop the invasion, but their nationalism would not allow them to transform into Villistas. They decided instead to confront Pershing. On more than one occasion these confrontations produced casualties and prisoners on both sides. Unfortunately for Villa, each time, presidents Carranza and Wilson managed to keep the situation from escalating into a war.

VILLISMO AT ITS NADIR

Regardless of Villa's rising hopes, he continued to face enormous odds. General Pershing's expedition gave him a reason to fight, helping him to attract new volunteers. However, volunteers were not nearly as numerous as before. He had failed to provoke the nationwide anti-Carrancista uprising he had hoped for. In addition, Villa had always depended on U.S. support and now practically no American was willing to help him. Villa had no alternative but to seek supplies by stealing them from Carrancista troops.

The two and a half months following Pershing's invasion were probably the most difficult time for Villa and Villismo. He ordered General Nicolas Fernandez to take his troops to Durango and lay low. The rest of his officers faced harder conditions in Chihuahua. Pershing captured or killed several of them. One of the most notorious, Candelario Cervantes, tried to hide in Namiquipa, but the villagers, who respected Pershing, gave away Cervantes's hideout. He was captured and his troops destroyed. Another of Villa's senior generals, Calixto Contreras, was killed when he tried to surrender to Carrancistas after failing to find a place to hide. Pablo Lopez, who had directed the massacre at Santa Isabel and participated in the Columbus raid, found himself on the run. He was injured in early June and hid in a cave to recover from his wound. The Carrancistas found him when his assistant left the shelter to look for food and medicine. Lopez was arrested and executed. His last wishes were to not have any Americans present and, in a show of enormous courage, he asked to give the orders for his own execution to the firing squad.

Villa's Cave

Villa himself managed to elude the Punitive Expedition, but he was incapable of fighting for anything more than much-needed supplies. One of his luckiest moments in these dark months occurred on March 27, 1916 when Villa attacked both the Miñeca garrison and Ciudad Guerrero. He captured a load of 30,000 cartridges from the garrison. In the city, Villa also managed to capture a large amount of ammunition and welcomed 80 captured Carrancistas into his militia.

This lucky moment also produced one of the most dangerous episodes in Villa's already dangerous life. During the attack at Ciudad Guerrero, a bullet hit Villa below his right knee, getting stock in the shattered bone. Villa's wound was very serious. The pain was so intense that it made it impossible for him to ride his horse. This immobility kept him from directing any attacks and made him an easier target. He was forced to disperse his troops into smaller gangs and to find a place to hide and heal.

During these trying times for Villismo, Villa was forced into seclusion in a cave known as Cozcomate. The cave was near Jose Rodriguez's ranch. Rodriguez was a Villista general who had recently been killed, but his father, who lived on the ranch, offered Villa assistance. Villa's wound became infected because he had no medicine to treat it. The infection produced enormous pain and, at times, hallucinations. He had a couple of assistants with him but very limited food and water, and no medicine. Every third day or so, one of his assistants had to leave the cave to come down the cliff and obtain water and food. Regardless of these hardships, Villa managed to remain undetected. On April 11, he was able to see from his cave the camp of one of Pershing's convoys. This would be the closest the expedition ever got to him, but, unaware of this, the convoy proceeded on its way toward Parral.

Villa became aware of rumors of his death. He tried to encourage such rumors so General Pershing would declare the U.S. mission accomplished and leave Mexico. Villa ordered his men to dig graves and bury cattle carcasses at different locations and spread the word that he was buried there. The trick did not have the desired effect. Many Mexicans believed that Villa was in fact dead. Even Carrancista generals believed Villa was dead and pressured Carranza to expel the U.S. troops from Mexico. But Pershing needed proof and did not leave the country.

President Wilson negotiated with Carranza and received an extension for the expedition to remain in Mexico. Wilson proposed that the U.S. forces would leave Mexico if the United States retained the right to send troops back again to protect U.S. lives and property. A similar policy, known as the Roosevelt Corollary to the Monroe Doctrine, was being used in the Caribbean and Central America and resulted in a number of U.S. military occupations. Carranza considered this an insult to Mexican sovereignty and refused. President Wilson tried to pressure Carranza by expanding the economic embargo to include Mexican exports, but Carranza did not cave in. In the meantime, tensions between U.S. and Mexican forces in Chihuahua escalated, bringing the two countries to the brink of war. Once again, the presidents were not interested in war and managed to defuse the situation. President Wilson agreed to limit the reach of the expedition to no further than 200 miles from the border. This limitation finally allowed Villa to leave the cave.

THE RETURN OF VILLA

Villa emerged from hiding right before Pershing managed to destroy his entire movement. Rumors about Villa's death had been so consistent that even Villistas began to believe that their boss was dead. Nicolas Fernandez, who managed to keep most of his troops intact in Durango, was considering surrender. However, he had previously agreed with Villa to reconvene all the forces in Durango by July 1, so Fernandez decided to wait. In the meantime, Villa's infection had spread all the way down to his foot. This made any travel extremely painful, but missing the deadline would have meant the end of Villismo. Villa traveled on a stretcher made out of a little cart pulled by a horse. Once in Durango, he assessed the situation. His troops had been severely weakened but not destroyed. He sent his most trusted men to retrieve some of the hidden money, weapons, and ammunition. These supplies were not enough to recreate the Division of the North, but they were enough to revive his guerrilla army.

After saving Villismo, the most urgent task was for Villa to seek medical attention. He sought the assistance of a nurse who treated his wound. She controlled the infection, but could not operate, leaving the bullet in the bone. Villa would spend the months of July and August regaining the use of his leg and coordinating his men to engage in sneak attacks aimed at taking supplies from Carrancistas.

On July 3, 1916, the Villistas made their first attack on a small Carrancista unit near Rio Florido. Two days later, they attacked the town of Jimenez where they collected more weapons and ammunition. At every opportunity Villa spoke to villagers about their duty to join him. He continued insisting that the enemy was the invading U.S. forces, although people began to notice that Villa attacked only Carrancistas. Some followed him, but still there was no massive recruitment reminiscent of Villa's golden years. Villa saw the need once more to force conscription in order to increase the size of his militias. This made him increasingly unpopular in his own state. Villagers slipped away and went into hiding every time they saw Villistas approaching their towns. Desertions increased among those forced to join him, especially when they realized that they were fighting Carrancistas and not Pershing's troops.

Not all was despair for Villa, though. Many of the Villistas who had disbanded while Villa was hiding began to join him after receiving news of his return. Despite the enormous difficulties he had rebuilding his army, Villa was becoming a nightmare for the federal army. During the next two years of the revolution (1916–1917), the war desensitized the revolutionaries on both sides. They began committing merciless acts of brutality. All prisoners were now executed. Neither side showed interest in sparing the lives of those willing to join their cause. In addition, the bodies of the executed men were displayed, hanging from telegraph poles or trees, as a warning to others. This period was so callous that even those recovering from injuries in hospitals were executed in their beds.

Villa's Attack on Ciudad Chihuahua

By the end of August 1916, Villa had less than 1,000 troops and felt strong enough to try to regain control of Chihuahua. His first move in this direction was full of symbolism. He decided to attack Ciudad Chihuahua on the night of September 15, the night when Mexicans across the country celebrate Independence Day. By choosing this date, Villa was sending the message that Mexico was once again occupied by foreign forces and he was leading the movement to liberate the homeland. He showed enormous daring, warning General Jacinto B. Treviño, the military governor of Chihuahua, that he would lead the festivities in Ciudad Chihuahua's central plaza. General Treviño, who had 9,000 troops under his command, did not pay any attention to this threat. Treviño went ahead with his plan to celebrate independence and even allowed many of his officers to spread throughout the city to attend private celebrations.

General Treviño knew Villa was not strong enough to occupy the city, but he failed to recognize that Villa was not interested in permanently occupying the city. He just wanted to expose the ineptitude of the federal army and free important revolutionaries from the city's prison. Many Orozquistas housed in this prison had fought against Villa, but he hoped that, since the Punitive Expedition had recently killed Orozco, they would join him to avenge their leader. He was particularly interested in freeing Jose Ines Salazar, one of Orozco's most skilled generals.

As promised, Villa attacked Ciudad Chihuahua that night at 11:00 P.M. Despite his announced attack, he took the city's defenses by surprise. He concentrated his attack on two places, the prison and the governor's palace. Treviño was unable to organize any resistance, so he fled to Santa Rosa Hill, where he hoped he could put together some kind of defense, but to no avail. By midnight, Villa had the city under his control and was celebrating independence as promised. He also managed to free 80 prisoners, including General Salazar, incorporating them into his army.[2]

Villa had humiliated General Treviño without suffering many casualties. However, some of Villa's men made a fatal mistake. Those who stormed the prison fled the city, but those who stormed the governor's palace missed the signal to retreat. The next morning, General Treviño began the bombardment of the palace. The Villistas stationed there were soon surrounded and had no option but to fight their way out, suffering serious causalities.

Villa's Gains from His Success at Ciudad Chihuahua

Regardless of the late setback, Villa had succeeded in his two main goals at Ciudad Chihuahua and had demonstrated that he was still a force to be reckoned with. He embarrassed the federal army and acquired his most important experienced officers. He demonstrated that he could strike practically at will any important target in Chihuahua. The attack was an embarrassment, not only for the 9,000 Mexican troops, but also to the 10,000 U.S. soldiers deployed throughout the region to capture him. After this impressive victory, volunteers began joining Villa in the hope for resurgence.

The San Andres Manifesto

Three days later, Villa left Ciudad Chihuahua and arrived at the village of San Andres. He tricked the garrison's commander by sending a telegram pretending to be Colonel Zuazua. In the telegram, Villa indicated that the rumors that Villa was approaching his garrison were false. Thus, when Villa arrived, the garrison offered no resistance. Villa captured and executed all the soldiers.

In order to legitimize his new revival, Villa had to explain his goal. He published a manifesto formalizing his xenophobic feelings first announced at Naco and declaring his commitment to sending Pershing's Punitive Expedition out of Mexico. He added that he was fighting to keep the United States from appropriating border and coastal territory in Mexico. He singled out U.S. and Chinese nationals, declaring that their presence limited the possibility for Mexicans to find jobs and improve their economic situation. Mexican business and industry, he asserted, would thrive without this foreign competition. He declared that if captured they would be executed and their properties confiscated. Indeed, xenophobia would be the central theme of his new social and economic program. He appeared to have forgotten the revolution's central goal: social justice.

The *San Andres Manifesto* was in reality a subtle plot against Carranza. Villa had no interest in fighting Pershing, but he continued trying to utilize his presence to attract to his side those Carrancista officers who had objected to Carranza's lukewarm effort to expel U.S. soldiers from Mexican soil. The manifesto also guaranteed that only civilians could run for president, calming the anxieties of those Carrancistas who feared a Villa presidency. Furthermore, in order to weaken Carranza's centralized government and attract the support of regional strongmen, Villa promoted the idea of local and regional elections.

Villa's ability to come back had depended on his capacity to attract vast numbers of volunteers. The *San Andres Manifesto* failed to achieve just that because circumstances had changed. Carranza was considered the victor while fewer people than before were interested in joining Villa, who was obviously on the run and offered no clear revolutionary goals.

Villa: The Bloodthirsty Bandit

By the fall of 1916, Villa had become an angry and vengeful man, blaming everyone but himself for his defeats. Every time he occupied a town or village, he rounded up all men and forced them to give away their property or to join his army. In contradiction of the *San Andres Manifesto*, Villa continued his attacks on Carrancistas while avoiding any clash with U.S. troops. In the month of October, when he attacked the troops of Generals Cavazos and Ozuna, Villa showed no mercy. He killed everybody and exhibited the bodies by spreading them along the road.

Villa had become a dark version of his old Robin Hood image. Villa was only interested in punishing the rich without offering assistance for the poor. When he occupied the town of Parral, he ordered the arrest of all the sons of the town's wealthy citizens. He kept them corralled in a stockade and kept their food rationed to dried meat and corn. He told them that now "they had to live as the poor were living."[3] The prisoners and their families were terrified, not knowing if Villa would execute them or not. After several days, he simply freed them and left town. His new attitude did nothing for the poor. Terrified villagers became willing to die fighting in defense of their community rather than allowing the Villistas to rape their women, rob their food, and force them into conscription.

Villa developed an unquenchable thirst for vengeance. In one particular case, he attacked the town of Namiquipa. He accused the villagers of denying him support and giving preference to Pershing, who helped them create their *defensas sociales* that resisted him. In addition, he blamed the villagers for the death of Candelario Cervantes, one of his closest officers. When he arrived at the town on October 10, he allowed his troops to loot and engage in all sorts of abuses. What Villa did not seem to understand was that the more vengeful he became, the less chance he had to rebuild his Division of the North.

Villa's Resilience in Chihuahua

Villa's revolutionary appeal was seriously affected by his aggressive behavior, but was not completely destroyed. One reason for its resilience was the behavior of the Carrancista government in Chihuahua. Governor Treviño was corrupt and abusive, causing Chihuahuans to remember with nostalgia the times of Governor Villa. In order to keep control of the state, President Carranza had appointed Treviño precisely because he was not originally from Chihuahua. The idea was for his military governors to pacify their territories, but since they did not have local connections they could not become regional strongmen independent of Carranza. The unintended results were corrupt and abusive governments because many of these governors saw their appointments as opportunities for quick enrichment.

Even though he had shown ineptitude trying to stop Villa, Treviño had been fairly successful at self-enrichment and at terrorizing the population. He extracted revenues through all sorts of confiscations and tax schemes. His men arrested and even executed anyone they considered uncooperative. Not surprisingly, the decline in Villa's popularity was slowed by General Treviño's administrative practices.

Villa's Second Attack on Ciudad Chihuahua

Toward the end of 1916, an overly optimistic Villa believed that he was now capable of assuming permanent control of the state's capital. Indeed, his situation had improved. First, his leg had healed enough to allow him to lead his army. In October, he had gone to Parral, where a doctor operated on his leg and managed to extract the bullet that had remained embedded in the bone. After a brief recovery, Villa was finally able to ride his horse and fight with his men (although he continued limping and experiencing pain the rest of his life). Second, he had managed to increase the size of his army to some 1,500 troops, but Treviño had 4,000 soldiers and General Francisco Murguia had an additional 15,000 men stationed at Torreon, close enough to reinforce General Treviño's forces if necessary. Villa was not deterred by this. After all, it was under adversity that he had managed to win some of his most famous victories.

On November 23, Villa attacked Ciudad Chihuahua for the second time that year. He managed to surprise the first line of defense, but his lack of artillery weakened his offensive and kept his cavalry from reaching the enemy. After three days of resistance, Treviño was confident that he had successfully repelled Villa. His confidence was such that on November 26 he organized a party in celebration.

However, Villa was not yet defeated. He and his officers were still trying to figure out how to break Treviño's defenses. The answer arrived from an unexpected source. A 23-year-old soldier named Martin Lopez, wounded during the earlier stages of the battle, decided to leave his hospital bed and go to Villa's headquarters. Standing in front of Villa, still covered with bandages on his left arm and thorax, Lopez requested 300 men to help him lead an attack on Santa Rosa Hill to destroy Treviño's artillery. At first, Villa dismissed this as a crazy idea but Lopez insisted. Villa did not have many options, so he decided to give Lopez a chance. Minutes before midnight, as Treviño was celebrating his victory, Martin Lopez managed to approach the hill undetected and stormed it. He soon controlled the artillery and signaled Villa his success. Villa then proceeded to attack the city. By 7:00 A.M., Villa had full control of the state's capital. A shocked Treviño, and many of his officers, barely managed to escape. Martin Lopez became the hero of this attack and gained Villa's full confidence, respect, and affection. He became one of Villa's most important officers.

Perhaps expecting soon to govern the state again, Villa treated this victory with magnanimity reminiscent of the times when he was at the height of his power. He did not execute any of his prisoners and restrained his troops from looting the city. Instead, he spoke to the prisoners about his struggle against the U.S. invasion and asked them to join him. This rhetoric gave Villa certain legitimacy, but most people knew well that his real quarrel was with Carranza. The prisoners accepted Villa's offer in order to avoid the firing squad, but many of them rejoined Carranza at the first opportunity.

VILLA AND PERSHING'S PUNITIVE EXPEDITION

Villa's second consecutive success in Ciudad Chihuahua was another embarrassment for the Carranza and Pershing forces that were after him. Villa proved that his first attack was not luck and that they could not stop him. Pershing was furious. He made a request to President Wilson to take full control of Chihuahua, but the president remained reluctant. World War I was increasingly occupying most of his attention, and the last thing he needed was Pershing complicating the political situation in Mexico.

In the meantime, U.S. newspapers focused on the accomplishments of the Pershing Expedition rather than on its failure to capture Villa. To be sure, there was reason for celebration. During the 11 months that the expedition spent in Mexico, Pershing killed General Julio Cardenas, Villa's head of his Dorados elite unit, and other important officers, such as Colonel Candelario Cervantes.

However, the expedition got much closer to provoking a war with Mexico than to capturing Villa. Particularly dangerous were two incidents involving U.S. troops and the Mexican army: one at Parral and another at Carrizal. In these two incidents, Carrancista officers, dismayed at the presence of U.S. troops in Mexican territory, decided to confront the Americans. The resulting skirmishes resulted in the death and imprisonment of soldiers on both sides, bringing the two countries, once more, to the brink of war. And, once again, Presidents Wilson and Carranza skillfully diffused the crises.

U.S. Plot Against Villa's Life

Frustrated, U.S. officials began considering assassination as the only way to get rid of Villa. The plot was led by the Bureau of Investigation (predecessor to the Federal Bureau of Investigation—FBI). The Bureau got in contact with members of the Japanese community in Chihuahua. In contrast to his feelings for the Chinese, Villa respected the Japanese people and some had become close to him. Two of them, Dyo and Fusita, were hired by the U.S. agency to pour poison into Villa's coffee. However, Villa always expected assassination attempts and his daily routine was designed to avert them. He was aware of the possibility of poisoning, so he always had someone tasting his food and drinks before him. When Dyo and Fusita saw Villa giving part of his poisoned coffee to a soldier they panicked and left the camp. It is unclear what happened afterward. Perhaps the poison was too weak to kill or perhaps the soldier showed signs of poisoning before Villa drank his coffee. In any event, Villa survived.[4]

The Aftermath of the Punitive Expedition

Regardless of its gains against Villismo, the Punitive Expedition was in many aspects a failure. It was an embarrassment for the U.S. army, as people in the United States, Mexico, and Europe witnessed the inability of the U.S. government to capture a single man. This was welcome news for a Germany concerned with the consequences of the United States assisting the Allied Forces in World War I.

The expedition also damaged Carranza's reputation. In particular, the 11-month presence of the expedition in Mexico weakened Carranza's approval among his generals. He found it extremely difficult to maintain his image as the uncompromising defender of Mexican sovereignty while allowing U.S. forces to roam freely in Chihuahua. More dangerous for Carranza was the increasing belief that perhaps Villa was right about Carranza's plan to sell northern Mexico to the United States.

Ironically, the person who benefited the most from the Punitive Expedition was Villa. From the moment the expedition entered Mexico on March 15, 1916, until it withdrew on February 7, 1917, it provided him with justification to continue fighting. The killing of important Villista officers aside, Villa's most difficult time during this period was the result of his injured leg, which had little to do with the Punitive Expedition. His ability to hide and then to reappear over and over again only demonstrated the incompetence of Pershing's and Carranza's armies. Many Mexicans began to believe that Villa's comeback was inevitable. Unfortunately for Villa, the departure of the Punitive Expedition led to his steady decline.

VILLA'S LAST COMEBACK

After the *Naco Manifesto*, Villa had justified his fight by promoting the need to get rid of the U.S. invaders. Once the Pershing expedition left, Villa's personal quarrel with Carranza was exposed as his real reason to continue fighting.

Villa and Zapata had rejected Carranza from the beginning because they considered him just another ambitious member of the Mexican elite with no real revolutionary credentials. They believed he was determined to become a dictator and his presidency was confirming their suspicions. President Carranza continuously obstructed the main goals of the revolution, such as land reform, workers' rights, and democracy. He had remained determined to return the large haciendas confiscated by the revolution back to their prerevolutionary owners. He grew increasingly intolerant of workers' strikes and their demands for better working conditions. Unlike for Madero, democracy did not appear among Carranza's priorities. He showed little tolerance for opposition candidates. Most of them were unjustifiably removed from the ballots or harassed by government agents. He imposed his preferred candidates on the Mexican populace and denied the principles of local autonomy. Villa could have benefited from exposing Carranza's authoritarian attitude as much as he had benefited from Treviño's corruption in the state of Chihuahua, but his struggle became a stubborn personal quest against Carranza. Many Mexicans were tired of so many years of war and economic decline, and Villa offered nothing more than the continuation of fighting and suffering. He failed to inspire volunteers, and his expected resurgence failed to materialize in 1917, precisely because of public weariness of war and hardship.

Retreating from Chihuahua

Villa's victory at Ciudad Chihuahua brought optimism to his camp, but it turned out to be a short-lived victory. As soon as news of the fall of the state's capital reached Carranza, he ordered General Francisco

Murguia to challenge Villa. Murguia was not Treviño. He had fought with Obregon in the Battles of Celaya and Aguascalientes. Not only did he know how to defeat Villa, but unlike Treviño, he showed more determination in destroying Villa than in self-glorification and self-enrichment. He was also a ruthless general capable of doing anything to uproot Villismo. He became known as "Pancho Mecates" (Pancho Ropes) for his habit of leaving the bodies of executed Villistas hanging in trees and from telegraph poles. This was his warning to those considering joining or assisting Villa. Perhaps because of Murguia's ruthless determination, Villa showed a rare respect for him. Once he learned that Murguia was approaching Ciudad Chihuahua, Villa did not consider resisting and began preparations to evacuate the city.

Before leaving, Villa tried to collect as many resources as possible, but Murguia's 10,000 troops were moving too fast. Trying to gain time, Villa decided to send a detachment of 3,000 men to slow Murguia down. Jose Ines Salazar, one of the Orozquistas recently liberated by Villa, commanded this mission. Regardless of his inferior numbers, Salazar demonstrated his value as a general. He managed to keep his troops well-disciplined while harassing Murguia's men. Murguia was forced to delay his advance for three days, allowing enough time for Villa to take all he could.[5] On December 4, Villa watched Murguia enter the city. Villa was disappointed and furious but did not lose hope. At this moment Villa simply muttered, "I'd trade you Chihuahua for Torreon," and headed for the famous commercial hub.[6]

Villa remained convinced that he could take control of the whole state of Chihuahua again, as he had done in 1913. Once again, he expected to resupply his troops at Torreon. On his way there, he split from his army with a few of his most trusted men and went to the hacienda of Chavarria, one of the many places where in 1915 he had hidden money, weapons, and ammunition. With these supplies, the Villistas were ready to take Torreon.

The Massacre at Camargo

Villa managed to get rid of Murguia's pursuing forces by using empty trains as decoys while his forces marched far from the railroad tracks. Villa then attacked the town of Camargo to get some more supplies.

He took the defenders by surprise and captured the garrison without much difficulty. However, an incident in this town shattered Villa's already weak reputation as the Robin Hood of the revolution and increased his image as the bloodthirsty bandit. Villa was certainly not the only one. Years of constant warfare increased the level of brutality on both sides. But Carranza's propaganda machine was more effective at promoting Villa's negative image, and the massacre at Camargo helped to reinforce it.

Indeed, at Camargo, Villa crossed a new threshold of brutality. Executions of prisoners, including injured soldiers in their hospital beds, were by now fairly common. Even General Murguia made a name for himself for his hangings, but no one until this moment had executed women en masse. As Villa occupied the village, a woman approached him begging for her husband's life. An exasperated Villa told her that her husband had already been executed. The woman went into a rampage, screaming and insulting him, demanding also to be killed. Villa pulled out his gun and shot her on the spot. Sudden rage could, somehow, explain this act, but it is unclear what caused Villa's next action. He ordered the execution of all captured *soldaderas* (female soldiers); some 90 women were executed.[7] The grisly scene produced an enormous outcry even among Villa's closest supporters.

The Capture of Torreon

After the massacre at Camargo, Villa continued to Torreon. The city was defended by only 2,000 men under the command of General Severiano Talamantes. Obregon, as secretary of war, ordered Murguia to send troops to assist Talamantes, but he refused. Murguia assumed that, after leaving Torreon, Villa would return to Chihuahua, and he was preparing his defenses. Murguia calculated that the fall of Torreon would not strengthen Villa enough to take Ciudad Chihuahua, and he expected to destroy the Villista forces and become the hero who killed Villa. Obregon would have none of that and ordered Murguia to send troops, but he refused.

Villa attacked Torreon on December 21, 1916, and three days later he was in possession of the city. General Talamantes, unable to defend the city, decided to kill himself. Luis Herrera, a former member of the

Division of the North, also died defending the city. Villa ordered someone to fetch his body and hang it at the station with a one-peso bill
in one hand and a picture of Carranza in the other.[8] This was another
gruesome warning against those who had betrayed him. Herrera's family never forgave him for this.

As Villa had expected, Torreon still contained plenty of resources
and weapons to reinforce his army. In addition, he found gold and silver from Santa Barbara Station and money in the garrison from the
troops' payroll. Villa became convinced that the Battle of Torreon was
the beginning of his revival. This victory attracted, once more, enough
volunteers, putting him slightly short of Murguia's 8,000 men. As Murguia had hoped, Villa felt strong enough to try his new army at Ciudad
Chihuahua.

The Battle at Reforma Station

Villa confronted Murguia's advancing forces at the outskirts of the capital at the Reforma Train Station. On January 3, 1917, the confrontation
between these two large armies brought back memories of the massive
battles of the 1914–1915 campaigns. Villa was confident that one massive cavalry charge would destroy Murguia. However, most of Murguia's
men were well-seasoned soldiers who had defeated Villa in 1915. They
knew how to resist his charges and counterattacks. By contrast, most of
Villa's experienced officers had left him, and his current officers were
mainly guerilla fighters with limited experience in formal combat. Villa
did not see this as a reason for caution and ordered a massive cavalry
charge. The attack failed to break the defenses and, as in Celaya and
Leon, Murguia responded with a counterattack. Villa once again had
neglected to leave a reserve and was unable to resist Murguia's offensive. Villa was forced to retreat, wasting his last serious opportunity to
rebuild his Division of the North.

Villa tried to gather his forces at Parral, but the disorganization of
the retreat made it difficult to defend that position, and he was forced
to retreat even further. As he was leaving Parral, Villa did not have
time to organize the withdrawal of his 14 trains loaded with supplies.
Abandoning the trains would have strengthened Murguia, so Villa decided to let the villagers take everything they could. This action, and

the limited violence that the people of Parral experienced from Villistas, made this town a long-lasting stronghold of Villismo. Being on the run without the necessary supplies, Villa was forced to disband his army one last time. Villa's hope for a comeback vanished.

The Battle at Rosario Station

Murguia tried to deliver the final blow to Villa. However, as had already happened many times, Villa was at his best when he was weak and vulnerable, perhaps because he became more measured and cautious, avoiding risky engagements with the enemy. Murguia chased Villa and confronted him in early March near the Rosario Train Station. This time Villa trusted Martin Lopez to lead an offensive. Murguia's 5,000 men were double the number of Lopez's, so a direct confrontation was out of the question. Instead, Villa ordered Lopez to simulate an attack and a retreat. While Murguia forces engaged Martin Lopez, Villa ordered Baudelio Uribe to encircle Murguia. The scheme worked. Murguia believed that he had defeated Martin Lopez so he began pursuing his men. Uribe's attack from the rear took Murguia by surprise, costing him half of his men. He was lucky that a Villista did not recognize him. The Villista believed he was a low-ranking officer and simply hit the general with his sword, humiliating him, but not capturing him. Villa won the day and promptly executed all 600 prisoners. This time, due to lack of ammunition, he replaced firing squads with executions by single shots to the head.[9] After this humiliating defeat, Murguia briefly considered suicide. Villa, in the meantime, reoccupied Parral and other small garrisons abandoned by Murguia's retreating forces.

The Betrayal of Rafael Mendoza

Villa believed that he could destroy Murguia and regain full control of Chihuahua. This time, his men's morale was high while Murguia's forces were completely demoralized. Villa was running short of ammunition, but he had time to resupply from a stockpile he had hidden at the hacienda of Chevarria.

Unfortunately, one of his confidants, Major Rafael Mendoza, ruined Villa's plan. Mendoza was a member of Villa's personal guard who, in 1915, had helped him hide the weapons he was planning to retrieve.

During the last battle, Mendoza was wounded in his foot so he went home to heal. While still recovering, he went on a drunken rampage, getting the attention of some Carrancistas who recognized him and captured him. Murguia ordered Mendoza hanged. The Villista lost his nerve and begged Murguia to spare his life. In exchange, he promised to lead Murguia to Villa's weapons hideout. This way, Villa lost the valuable ammunition he was counting on to destroy Murguia.

Villa Attacks Ciudad Chihuahua for the Third Time

Villa, however, decided to continue his plan to take Ciudad Chihuahua. Villa was considering engaging this very important battle with limited ammunition, but he was overconfident that his forces could carry the day. In April 1917, he attacked Ciudad Chihuahua for the third time since the dissolution of the Division of the North. General Murguia had remained in command of the garrison. Both Villa and Murguia had about 2,000 men each, but Obregon was sending 5,000 additional troops that were rapidly approaching the city. Villa was facing a shortage of ammunition and limited time, so he decided to bet his luck on a massive concentrated charge to rapidly penetrate Murguia's defenses. Unfortunately for Villa, Murguia, familiar with Villa's tactics, contained the attack long enough to exhaust Villa's ammunition. Villa had no alternative but to retreat. A reinforced Murguia took the offensive and defeated the poorly armed and exhausted Villistas. He captured 200 prisoners, hanging 43 of them in the trees of the city's Columbus Avenue.

The Rape of Namiquipa

Villa was furious and desperately tried to find a culprit for this military failure. His scapegoat was Major Rafael Mendoza for giving away his weapons depot and fighting against him with Murguia's army. Mendoza was a resident of Namiquipa, so Villa decided to teach Mendoza a lesson by attacking his hometown. The town had nothing to do with his quarrel with Mendoza, but Villa also resented these villagers' collaboration with General Pershing. It was in this town that Pershing established the first *defensas sociales* that had been troubling Villa for the past two years. Villa made up his mind and decided to release his wrath on Namiquipa.

As Villa approached Namiquipa, the men ran to the hills. Villa was frustrated that he could not teach a lesson to the defenders of the town, so he broke once more the unwritten law regarding women's wartime immunity. He ordered all the women captured and then ordered his men to rape them after setting the town ablaze. Villa's thirst for revenge was satisfied, but his reputation as a bloodthirsty revolutionary was sealed.

News of the rapes at Namiquipa caused villagers from other towns to fear Villa and to collaborate with the federal army. This situation was very dangerous for Villa. His ability to survive with a small militia for the past two years had depended on the support that he received from villagers throughout Chihuahua. They had provided invaluable intelligence to help him hide while being aware of his enemies' moves and providing false intelligence to confuse his enemies. Villagers had shared their meager resources to help feed Villa's troops. After Namiquipa, he and his men were practically on their own. In the midst of this dire situation, another determined general, Joaquin Amaro, and his 1,200 troops were assigned to chase and destroy Villa. Villa was forced to disband his army.

Anger and merciless acts were the result of Villa's incapacity to regain his previous glory. More of his men lost hope and decided to leave him. The few who decided to stay with him formed small bands that depended on hit-and-run strategies to steal food and weapons from small garrisons or villages. They were simply trying to stay alive. Carranza believed that Villa was finished and it was only a matter of time before he was either captured or killed. However, Villa continued demonstrating extraordinary abilities to do the unthinkable and reemerged over and over again.

Villa's Plan to Kidnap Carranza

By the spring of 1917, Villa had reached his lowest point of popular support and, with the Pershing Punitive Expedition already out of Mexico, he had no obvious reason to continue fighting. But he was not one to give up as long as Carranza remained president of Mexico. Carranza, on his part, had consolidated his position as president of the country. Four issues helped him achieve this: all U.S. troops had left the country, Villa was militarily defeated, Carranza had been elected president of Mexico, and his promised revolutionary constitution was well received and soon to become the law of the land. Villa did not accept this and decided for the first time to directly target President Carranza.

Villa conceived a daring and unpredictable plan. In the summer of 1917, he decided to go to Mexico City, kidnap the president, and take him to Zapatista territory for trial. The task was far more difficult than Villa expected. This implied traveling through hundreds of miles of unfriendly territory, complicated by the fact that there was a bounty placed on his head and a growing number of Mexicans were willing to turn him in. Regardless, he hoped that he could go all the way to the heart of Mexico City and capture the president during one of his daily strolls in Chapultepec Park.

Villa sent Jose Maria Jaurrieta and Alfonso Gomez to Mexico City to begin the initial preparations for the kidnapping. They established a business as horse traders to avoid raising suspicions while collecting intelligence about the president's routine and his security. In the mean-time, Villa led 100 men on horseback to Mexico City. He took them through back country to avoid detection. Out of Chihuahua, Villa was in unfriendly territory and could trust no one. He used local guides and killed them as he moved along to the next leg of the journey. He had to keep his face hidden by pushing his hat down or covering his lower face by wrapping a poncho around his shoulders. In addition, his expedition was constantly harassed by *defensas sociales* who considered the group to be bandits. The expedition was too large to feed and to keep unnoticed, so he decided to send half of his men back to Chihua-hua. Things did not get any easier. The lack of support from the local population meant that they had to endure thirst and hunger and often lost their way. A stubborn Villa refused to give up, but many of his men lost hope and began to desert him. The level of desperation was such that in early August he finally decided to call off his plan. This was not the end of the ordeal. The way back became even more difficult. After much suffering, he returned exhausted, malnourished, and in rags, with only four men by his side. The plan was a total failure. Carranza was unaware of Villa's plot and never interrupted his daily stroll in the park.

Villa Running Out of Options

Villa continued looking for reasons to fight. His original struggle for social justice had been transformed into acts of banditry necessary to stay alive. For most of 1917 and 1918, Villa's actions were nothing more than random skirmishes against federal troops with practically no strategic purpose. One of the best known encounters of this period is his attack on the border town of Ojinaga on November 20, 1917. He combined day and night attacks to easily capture the garrison. Most of the defenders desperately ran into the United States for protection. Villa had hoped to capture some weapons and ammunition and utilize this location to smuggle weapons from the United States, but the garrison turned out to be poorly supplied and did not satisfy Villa's needs. In addition, while Villa had gold and silver, mainly acquired through "security taxes" that he charged U.S. miners and businessmen for "protection," he found no one from across the border willing to sell him weapons. Disappointed, he and his men vanished, once again, into Chihuahua's countryside.

FELIPE ANGELES OFFERS VILLA A NEW REASON TO FIGHT

Since 1915 Villa had been incredibly resilient, but every effort to regain his successes of 1913–1914 had failed. He had been reduced to the status of a famous bandit. He had become increasingly brutal and had no clear justification to continue fighting. His resilience can be attributed to the fact that he had no alternative. He did try to surrender on a few occasions. The most notorious one was after his last defeat in Ciudad Chihuahua. He wrote to General Murguia suggesting the possibility of surrender, but Murguia was not interested. As far as he was concerned, Villa was a bandit and had to be punished for his long list of crimes. Villa had no alternative but to continue fighting without any realistic hope of ever defeating Carranza.

In the early summer of 1918, Felipe Angeles brought new hope to Villa. Angeles was poor and isolated, living in his ranch in the United States, but he was convinced that Mexico's problems originated with the assassination of Madero and that only by removing Carranza, installing real democratic reform, and establishing a policy of reconciliation could the country be healed. He believed that he was the only man capable of doing that and he was not alone in his thinking. Many exiled revolutionaries visited him trying to convince him to lead a new revolutionary alliance.

With this in mind, Angeles made arrangements to meet with Villa in January 1919 at Tosesihua. Reminiscing on better times, they fondly addressed each other as "my general." After an affectionate embrace, they began talking about the prospects for Villismo in the near future. Villa had high hopes for this meeting. He believed that this could be the answer to his elusive resurgence, but soon he was disappointed and shocked when he heard Angeles's plan to bring all revolutionary factions together. During his recent incursion into central Mexico, Villa had learned how difficult it was to move outside Chihuahua, much less roam the country trying to gather leaders to oppose Carranza. Instead, Villa suggested a plan to rebuild the Division of the North. Angeles, often perceived as the man who brought the best out of Villa, agreed to help him to do that as a first stage of his plan. He reasoned that a strong Villa could better help achieve his plan for reconciliation. This strategy looked promising. News of the Villa-Angeles alliance brought hope to many former Villistas and within a few months his army rapidly grew from a few hundred to 2,000 men.

Angeles brought back the old benevolent Villismo to his army. He convinced Villa that executions and revenge only alienated potential supporters so, during the next few battles, Villa showed more compassion. He freed his prisoners and stopped most executions. There was only one important exception at the town of Parral. In December 1918, Villa stormed this town and captured 85 prisoners. He freed all but three: the leader Jose Herrera and two of his younger sons. He was the father of Maclovio and Luis Herrera, two high-ranking Villistas who had abandoned him in 1915 to join Carranza. Luis was the man Villa had dug out of his grave and hanged at Torreon. Villa also believed that their father had betrayed him. He captured and executed him together with two more sons. They died in front of a firing squad yelling profanities at Villa. The only surviving son, Jesus, swore to avenge his family and kill Villa. He would fulfill his promise four years later.

Villa's Last Battle at Ciudad Juarez

An invigorated Villa decided to try once more to repeat his success of 1913 by attacking Ciudad Juarez in June 1919. As he prepared his attack, he moved his troops in a way that suggested that he was getting ready to storm Ciudad Chihuahua and thus leave Ciudad Juarez unprepared. He then maneuvered to attack the border town from the east and not from the more convenient south. The intention was to keep bullets from flying into El Paso and avoid another U.S. intervention. The attack began on June 15 and was commanded by Martin Lopez. They quickly managed to break the defenses and take over the city. However, Lopez failed to control his troops, who soon began looting the town. The fleeing federal forces became aware of the mayhem in the city and took advantage of it. The disbanded Villistas in the town were not prepared for the counterattack and were forced to abandon the city. Villa decided to storm the city once more, but this time he personally led the attack. Once again, the Villistas broke the defenses and forced the federal forces to flee. In an effort to assist the Carrancistas, U.S. troops across the border claimed that two U.S. citizens were killed by flying bullets and crossed the border to attack Villa. Villa was unable to fight the superior U.S. forces and was forced again to abandon the city.

Villa once again swore vengeance against all U.S. citizens in Chihuahua. Angeles was convinced that any hope for peace and reconciliation in Mexico required the cooperation of the U.S. government, but he was unable to stop Villa from expressing his anti-American rhetoric. Frustrated, he decided to leave Villa once and for all.

The Death of Felipe Angeles

Angeles continued with his plan to create a revolutionary alliance. Villa warned him that by roaming the countryside on his own he risked being captured and executed by Carrancistas. Angeles did not pay attention to this warning. For the next several months, he wandered endlessly throughout the countryside, unable to work out alliances.[10] As Villa had predicted, he was captured. In fact, he was betrayed. In November, Felix Salas, who had been part of his small escort, exposed his whereabouts to Carrancista forces in exchange for 6,000 pesos.

Carranza decided to court-martial Angeles and execute him as soon as possible. This was an illegal procedure since Angeles had not been a member of the federal army for several years, but Carranza needed to bring some air of legality to his execution. He was trying to avoid repeating the blunder of Zapata's assassination a few months earlier that had portrayed him as a murderer acting above the law. Angeles's lawyers requested a civilian trial, but it was denied. However, his court-martial became a soapbox from which Angeles addressed all Mexicans.

Unfortunately for Carranza, Angeles's eloquence gained him the sympathy of the public. He explained the reasons that forced him to join the revolution. He declared that the poor fought because they continued being exploited and were not protected by the law. He voiced what most Mexicans were quietly demanding: the need for peace and unity. He did not justify the atrocities committed by Villa, but demonstrated that Carranza had committed similar atrocities. His words expressed the sentiments of many Mexicans when he declared that neither Villa nor Carranza had been able to respond to people's demands for peace and liberty. His rhetoric attracted the support of millions of Mexicans, but the military judges, following instructions from Mexico City, promptly sentenced him to death. National and international observers demanded that Carranza issue a presidential pardon, but he refused. Angeles was executed on November 26, 1919. Thousands of people joined the funeral procession, protesting Carranza's injustice. Two days later, Villa avenged the death of his dear friend in an action that Angeles himself would have disapproved. He killed all the men defending the garrison at Santa Rosalia.[11]

VILLA RETIRING AS A REVOLUTIONARY

After Angeles's execution, Villa had not only lost a friend, but also his last justification for fighting as General Joaquin Amaro stepped up his efforts to capture him. Carranza believed that Villa's days were numbered. Neither Villa nor Carranza was interested in peace negotiations with each other. Only the death of one of them could end this impasse.

The Plan of Agua Prieta

Ironically, some of the most anti-Villista generals gave Villa his first real opportunity for amnesty. This had nothing to do with him, but with the presidential succession. Carranza's term in office was set to expire late in 1920, so different candidates were getting ready for the election. According to the new constitution, Carranza was not eligible for re-election. However, he was reluctant to give up power because he was afraid that General Obregon, the most powerful and popular of his generals, could become president, thus effectively transferring civilian power to the military. Consequently, Carranza tried to impose his own civilian candidate. He promoted the candidacy of Ignacio Bonilla, an obscure bureaucrat with no real political base. Everybody saw him as Carranza's future puppet president. In April 1920, at the town of Agua Prieta, General Obregon denounced Carranza's scheme and organized an anti-Carranza military alliance.

Villa realized that the break between Carranza and his generals could give him a new opportunity. Contrary to Villa's expectations, Obregon's plan was widely supported by the army so Villa could not appear as a second alternative for those generals dissatisfied with a Carranza-Obregon quarrel. On the contrary, the *Plan of Agua Prieta* turned Obregon into a formidable political force. Carranza realized his precarious situation and decided to escape to Veracruz, just as he had done during the Convention of Aguascalientes. However, on May 21, en route to his internal exile, he was betrayed by one of his bodyguards and killed near the town of Tlaxcalantongo.

Villa Negotiating Amnesty

Now that his nemesis was dead, Villa again sought amnesty. However, most of the leaders of Agua Prieta (Generals Alvaro Obregon, Plutarco E. Calles, and Benjamin Hill) had fought against Villa and they could hardly wait to capture and execute him. Only one of the plan's leaders, General Adolfo de la Huerta, had no real grievance against Villa. He never fought against him. On the contrary, he had been the man in charge of sending Villa the money he used to return from his exile back in 1913. The main leader of the plan was Obregon, but de la Huerta had been appointed interim president after Carranza's assassination. His main task was to arrange the presidential election to allow Obregon to assume the presidency by democratic means, but de la Huerta was interested in doing more as interim president than just that.

President Adolfo de la Huerta Reaches Out to Villa

President Adolfo de la Huerta was determined to appear as the man who brought peace to Mexico by offering a general amnesty that encouraged rebels to lay down their weapons. He reached out to Villa and proposed peace negotiations.

Unfortunately for Villa, President de la Huerta had a lot more convincing to do. As he was preparing to negotiate with him, the governor of Chihuahua, General Ignacio Enriquez, increased the reward for Villa's head to 100,000 pesos, while General Amaro intensified his efforts to capture him. With Zapata and Carranza dead, Villa was practically the last of the most important rivals. The leaders of Agua Prieta believed that getting rid of Villa would allow them to assume full control of the country.

Unaware of the schemes against him, Villa responded to the president's offer and sent some representatives to begin peace negotiations. De la Huerta assigned General Calles to represent the government. Villa was not present because he feared being betrayed and assassinated like Zapata and Carranza. His conditions for surrender included retaining his rank as general and being in charge of Chihuahua's armed forces, including the *defensas sociales* and the *Rurales*. Calles refused to grant any military powers to Villa. Instead, he suggested that Villa move to Sonora with a small armed escort. Villa refused because he would have become too vulnerable, living unprotected in an unfriendly state.

Only after the negotiations with Calles did Villa find out that Governor Enriquez and General Amaro were determined to get rid of him. Villa protested to President de la Huerta, who ordered Enriquez to declare void the reward for Villa's head and Amaro to suspend his manhunt. Villa regained his trust in the president and accepted another round of talks. This time Governor Enriquez arranged a face-to-face meeting. They both brought their armies but approached each other with only a white flag and a 15-man escort. After they greeted each other, they walked away from their escorts to talk in private. Almost immediately, Villa became agitated and left Enriquez. It turned out that Enriquez was not representing the federal government. In fact, this was his plan to kill Villa. After they both left for their respective camps, Enriquez began organizing a night raid on Villa's camp. Villa, however, became suspicious and left right away, leaving an empty camp that Enriquez attacked while Villa watched from a safe distance. Villa and President de la Huerta understood that they could not trust any of the generals to negotiate an amnesty.

General Francisco (Pancho) Villa. (Photo by Topical Press Agency/Getty Images.)

Villa's First Peace Agreement

Elias Torres, a journalist, was accepted by both parties to negotiate Villa's amnesty. On July 2, Villa met Torres in the hacienda of Encinillas. Villa's demands included keeping 500 *Rurales* and the hacienda of Horcasitas in Chihuahua. He was planning to use the hacienda to support his men and their widows. President de la Huerta refused the 500 *Rurales* and Villa living in Chihuahua, his stronghold, but he became hopeful that they could find an agreement. De la Huerta made a counteroffer, which included the hacienda of Canutillo in Durango and only 50 armed men for Villa's personal protection, insisting that Villa must become a civilian. He offered enough land to facilitate the retirement of 250 soldiers. Villa did not consider this enough but, having little alternative, he accepted. His only condition was that Generals Obregon, Calles, and Hill also sign the agreement. De la Huerta managed to convince Calles and Hill, but Obregon refused. He insisted that Villa had to pay for all his crimes.

The agreement meant Villa trusting his enemies and he understood the danger that this involved. In fact, Calles was playing a double game.

He had agreed with the president, but secretively he was considering options to kill Villa. In the meantime, Obregon, as minister of war, convinced de la Huerta of the high political price he would have to pay if the United States found out that he was negotiating with Villa. Villa learned about all this and cancelled the talks. In response, President de la Huerta authorized General Amaro to reinitiate his campaign against Villa.

Villa's Last Military Campaign

Villa was cornered and vulnerable. He understood that, in order to obtain a real amnesty, he had to negotiate from a position of strength. He decided to force the government to negotiate an amnesty or risk a prolonged bloody and costly war and he disappeared in mid-July. General Amaro tried to chase him, but he was incapable of finding his tracks. By the end of July, Villa emerged in the neighboring state of Coahuila and without any difficulties managed to occupy the garrison protecting the town of Sabinas. This was not only a simple military victory, but an amazing accomplishment of endurance and a strategic master stroke. To get to Sabinas, Villa led 100 men across 450 miles of the Bolson de Mapimi Desert. The task was so arduous that some of his men did not survive the crossing. However, once they arrived at Sabinas, they found plenty of food and water and also a new source of revenue to sustain his army. Coahuila had remained isolated from most of the devastation caused by the revolution; its haciendas were full of cattle and its businesses full of products and money. Villa threatened to transfer the war to Coahuila. This shocked the Mexican government as well as national and U.S. investors who had relied on this state as a safe region for economic development.

Villa Settles a Peace Agreement

Villa's plan worked. He was now in a stronger position to negotiate. As soon as Villa reappeared at Sabina, the president opened negotiations with him and managed to convince Generals Calles and Hill of the economic importance of stopping Villa from prolonging the war. Only two days later, the government and Villa signed a new peace agreement. The conditions were the same, except that this time Villa managed to get land for 850 of his soldiers.

Only Obregon continued refusing to sign the agreement. However, very quickly, he found himself isolated and portrayed by the media as the man who was refusing to secure peace in Mexico. Concerned with the upcoming presidential election in which he was the leading candidate, he caved in and accepted the conditions.

The formal armistice between Villa and the government took place on August 31, 1920 in Tlahualilo, Chihuahua. There, Villa and his men surrendered their weapons as Villa symbolically paid their last salary. Some of his men remained close to him, working in the two government-supplied haciendas located nearby Canutillo, Durango, the hacienda where Villa spent the rest of his life. Others accepted transfer to the federal army, while the rest took their pensions and joined civilian life. The following week, Villa peacefully retired from military life and settled down at Canutillo.

VILLA AT CANUTILLO

Villa lived anxiously his first three months at Canutillo. He was concerned that on December 1, 1920 Obregon was being sworn in as president. Villa was unsure if the new president would honor the peace agreement of Tlahualilo. However, Obregon kept his word and Villa began living in peace. In fact, they developed a friendship. Every now and then Villa and Obregon exchanged correspondence, and each letter reassured their mutual commitment to a long and lasting friendship.

The first year living in Canutillo was not easy for Villa. In its prerevolutionary years, Canutillo had been a prosperous hacienda of 163,000 acres, 4,400 of them irrigated. However, most of its infrastructure and wealth had been destroyed. Villa found the hacienda in ruins; only the chapel had a roof. All the cattle, horses, goats, and sheep were long gone and its arable land lay in ruins after not being cultivated for years.

Between 1921 and 1922, Villa's whole attention was devoted to bringing the hacienda back to its previous prosperity. He showed interest in acquiring modern machinery to increase the output of the land. He was particularly fond of machinery imported from the United States. He fixed and expanded the irrigation infrastructure and began rotating crops. Soon, he turned Canutillo into a successful business, mainly producing wheat, corn, and potatoes. He rebuilt its old structures and built four mills, one forge, and a post office. In addition, he opened telephone and telegraph lines connecting the hacienda to the town of Parral and built a new school.

Of all the improvements, he was particularly proud of the school. He named it "General Felipe Angeles," and it housed about 200 students. Most of them were children from the hacienda and nearby towns. Villa also encouraged adults to attend evening classes. Sometimes he sat in class to improve his own literacy skills. He started reading the *Treasure of the Youth*, "a kind of introductory book of knowledge for young people."[12]

During his first year at Canutillo, Villa retained the military discipline of his army. A bugle marked the different activities of the day from wakeup time to lights out, and his officers carried out daily reviews of troops. During this period, there were some unconfirmed rumors of executions of soldiers accused of robbery or insubordination.

By the second year, the discipline was somewhat relaxed, but Villa continued taking his personal security seriously. He was well aware that many people still wanted him dead. All his men were armed at all times, and patrols surveyed the hacienda. He also had people in nearby towns and train stations periodically reporting to him any suspicious activities.

Villa's old dream of building a military colony where workers created a self-sufficient cooperative and were militarily trained, was never implemented at Canutillo. In fact, Villa ran his hacienda following the same patron-worker relationship practiced by traditional hacendados. He provided land and seeds to peasants who paid him back with 1/3 of their crops. However, Villa ran the hacienda store in a very different manner. Instead of forcing his workers to incur debt with poor income and high prices, Villa sold them the products at cost and everything that was produced on his hacienda was offered to his workers free of charge.

Villa's Family Life

Villa used his peaceful years at Canutillo to bring order to his family life. Throughout his revolutionary years, Villa married many women. He did this to convince them that his romance was not a one-night stand. However, many of these weddings were fabricated. Sometimes he threatened judges to perform a wedding ceremony while ignoring his previous marriages; other times he had fake judges pretending to perform legitimate ceremonies. The result was that, by the time he retired to civilian life, Villa had over a dozen women claiming to be his legitimate wife. During the revolution, Villa acknowledged Luz Corral as his first and legitimate wife. Luz tolerated Villa's infidelities and marriages as long as he continued recognizing her as his primary wife.

Villa's love life was extremely active even beyond his multiple marriages. During the few months preceding the peace agreement alone, he had several informal love affairs from which he fathered three boys: Samuel with Maria Hernandez, Miguelito with Maria Arreola Hernandez, and Eleno with Maria Isaac Reyes.[13] The situation became even more complicated as he tried to bring some of his "official" wives to Canutillo. Soledad Seañez moved in with Villa and Luz Corral from the beginning. A few months later, Villa also brought Austreberta Renteria to live in the hacienda, and by 1922 Villa had Manuela Casas as his new girlfriend living in a hotel in nearby Parral.

Out of all these women, Austreberta became Villa's last love. For the first time since the beginning of the revolution, he refused to tolerate Luz Corral's condescending attitude toward his new lover. In fact, Villa replaced Luz with Austreberta in the main bedroom. Luz refused to give in and confronted her rival. Austreberta was so humiliated that she began crying. Villa noticed this and got so angry that he threw Luz out of Canutillo. Adding insult to injury, on October 27, 1922, Austreberta consolidated her position by giving Villa another son, Panchito.

Luz had been Villa's moral and emotional support for most of the revolution and now he simply abandoned her. An ungrateful Villa forgot all the sacrifices she endured supporting his revolutionary life. Left without economic support, Luz was forced to beg in order to survive. Sometimes she found help from Hipolito, Villa's brother. On other occasions, she managed to get some financial support from President Obregon.

THE ASSASSINATION OF PANCHO VILLA

Throughout most of his adult life, Villa knew many people had serious grievances against him and were determined to kill him. Therefore, his daily routine had always been full of rituals devoted to avoiding assassination attempts. In addition to changing sleeping places in the middle of the night and having someone tasting his meals before him, he never allowed anybody to walk behind him. Also, he always sat against walls to avoid being shot in the back.

Part of his safety depended on Villa's unpredictable routines, but settling down at Canutillo complicated things. That is why he kept Canutillo as a military fortress and had spies reporting directly to him. There, his survival depended mainly on the trust and protection of his men and the government. Not surprisingly, he assumed that at some point either Obregon or Calles, who had fought against him many times, could turn against him. However, as time passed, his friendship with President Obregon became stronger and Villa lowered his guard.

Jesus Herrera's Interest in Killing Villa

During his three years at Canutillo, Villa was the target of several assassination attempts, but he always managed to stay ahead of the game. One of his most determined enemies was Jesus Herrera, the last male survivor of the Herrera clan that Villa had so viciously tried to exterminate. Villa proved to be a very difficult target, which only reinforced Jesus's determination to kill him.

In October 1922, Herrera attempted his most daring plot against Villa to date. The plot received the support of Chihuahua's governor, Ignacio Enriquez. They sent a group of gunmen to Parral in order to survey the outskirts of Canutillo and seek an opportunity to kill him, but Villa was tipped off and ordered some of his men to go to Parral and befriend the gunmen. Villa's men got them drunk and took them to a brothel to kill them. Two were killed, but the rest managed to flee to Chihuahua. Among the survivors was Atenogenes Lopez, brother of Villa's cherished lieutenant, Martin Lopez. Atenogenes was wrongly convinced that Villa had had his brother killed and decided to join Herrera's efforts to kill him. Because of his peace agreement, Villa was unable to use force against Herrera, so he complained to President Obregon. The president contacted Herrera and assured Villa that his safety was guaranteed.

Villa Becomes a Political Liability

By the spring of 1923, the friendly relationship that had existed between Villa and Obregon suddenly changed. The political environment was reenergized by the presidential elections scheduled for the following year and Villa began to voice his political opinion. President Obregon was supporting the presidential candidacy of General Calles and became concerned about a politicized Villa. Villa tried to reassure everyone that he was not interested in politics while he naïvely suggested his preference for a de la Huerta presidency.

In the midst of this political environment, Regino Hernandez Llergo, from *El Universal* newspaper, arrived at Canutillo on May 28, 1923 and interviewed Villa for three days. Most of the interview focused on Villa's new life at Canutillo, but once in a while Hernandez Llergo asked political questions. Villa tried to make clear that he was not interested in taking up arms or politics. However, a few times in their long conversations, Villa contradicted himself. Once he hinted that he was interested in the governorship of Durango. Later on, concerned with the national perception that he was a defeated man, he boasted that he was still able to "mobilize 40,000 men in 40 minutes."[14] For people like Calles and Obregon, these comments meant trouble. Villa's possible support for de la Huerta's candidacy could complicate Calles's election or risk a new rebellion against the regime.

The Conspiracy

In March of 1923, Villa found out about another of Jesus Herrera's plans to kill him. Villa wrote to Obregon, who once again assured Villa that he had talked to Herrera and his security was guaranteed. Villa believed him. However, two months later, at Obregon's request, Herrera visited Calles in Mexico City and discussed ways to kill Villa.[15] Herrera assured Calles that all he needed was government protection for him and the assassins.

Herrera had found a man desperate enough to organize and lead the assassination. Meliton Lozoya had been the administrator of Canutillo before the revolution. He had only left the hacienda right before Villa moved in. He had taken everything he could and destroyed everything else in order not to leave anything to Villa. In May 1923, Villa learned about this and confronted him. Lozoya claimed that he had done so legally and under the orders of the owners of the hacienda. Villa gave him an ultimatum. Lozoya had one month to return all he took.[16] Lozoya was terrified. As far as he was concerned, the only way he could save his life was by killing Villa.

In the meantime, Calles, as minister of war, assigned General Joaquin Amaro the task of providing government support to the plotters. Jesus Salas Barraza, a representative of Durango's legislature, was Amaro's middleman to support Lozoya in anything he could need. Barraza was a curious choice. He did not appear to have any personal problem with Villa, but was fully committed to the plot.[17] Lozoya enlisted eight gunmen to do the job. In the meantime, Calles requested the presence of Colonel Felix Lara in Mexico City. Lara was the commander in charge of Parral's security, the town near Canutillo where the assassins planned to kill Villa. Calles told him about the plan to kill Villa and ordered him to clear the way for the assassins.[18]

The Assassination

Villa went to Parral regularly to visit his girlfriend, Manuela Casas, and to take care of business. On July 14, 1923, Villa left Canutillo to attend a baptism in Rio Florido. On his way back, he scheduled a stop in Parral. He was traveling by car with his secretary, Miguel Trillo, the driver, and four bodyguards. The assassins had rented two adjacent apartments on the second floor of a building at the intersection of Juarez and Barreda streets. It is believed that on July 19 a first attempt to kill him was foiled. As Villa passed the intersection, a group of children were crossing the street so the gunmen decided to hold their fire and wait for a better opportunity. Villa spent that night with Manuela.

In the early hours of July 20, the town's public works department dug a hole near the Juarez and Barreda intersection, partially blocking traffic. It is difficult to know if this was part of the plot, but it helped. At 5:00 A.M. that same morning, Colonel Lara took all his soldiers from Parral to the town of Maturna, arranging a rehearsal for the independence parade (two months ahead of time!). By 8:00 A.M., Villa left

Manuela's apartment and decided to drive the car himself. Trillo was in the passenger's seat, the driver on the running board, and the four bodyguards in the back seat. As they approached the intersection, Villa had to slow down because of the ditch and the mud from the dig. As he turned onto Barreda Street, a man took off his hat and yelled, "¡Viva Villa!" That was the signal. At least 40 bullets hit the car. Some people claimed as many as 150. Villa was hit with a dozen shots and died immediately. Trillo tried to react by pulling his gun as he was killed, leaving his body hanging backward from the passenger's window. One of the bodyguards was killed immediately; the other three managed to get out of the car. One of them killed one of the attackers as he escaped. The other two bodyguards were injured and managed to get away, but died soon after. The nation received the news of Villa's death in that day's afternoon papers. Mexicans were in shock and not sure if they could believe the news. While some celebrated, others mourned the end of one of the most widely known and significant leaders of the Mexican Revolution.

Obstruction of Justice

Following the assassination, the government did not attempt to take control of the situation. The attackers had the leisure to make sure that Villa was dead and they slowly rode away on their horses. They knew that everything had been prearranged and no one would chase them. The only policing body at Parral was Colonel Lara's garrison, but all his men remained out of town for several hours after the assassination. Once he received official notification of the assassination, he decided that there was nothing he could do. He argued that he had no horses to chase the assassins. He became notorious for such lame excuses during future interrogations. The government also failed to protect the scene of the crime. Curious people could roam freely around Villa's car, tampering with the evidence. Immediately after the assassination, a telegram was sent to President Obregon, informing him of Villa's death, but soon after the telegram was sent, the telegraph office at Parral was shut down. Villa's men did not learn about the murder for six hours. By then the assassins were long gone and there was little that Villa's men could do.

The Cover Up

To many national and international observers, the assassination of
Villa was clearly politically motivated and many believed that Calles
was behind it. President Obregon managed to stay out of any implications and tried to disassociate Calles from the killing in order to secure
his election. General Amaro used Salas Barrazas as a scapegoat and
thus distracted the attention from the presidential candidate. Having
given Amaro guaranteed government protection, Salas Barrazas wrote
a letter assuming full responsibility for the killing of Pancho Villa. He
declared he was the sole mastermind and, apart from his nine gunmen,
no one else was involved in the plot. He added that his motive was to
avenge all of Villa's victims. He was arrested and sentenced to 20 years
in prison. However, Amaro fulfilled his promise. After only six months,
Salas Barrazas was pardoned by the outgoing governor of Chihuahua,
General Ignacio Enriquez. Sometime later Salas Barrazas was promoted
to colonel and lived freely for the rest of his life. He died peacefully
30 years later.

Salas Barrazas's written confession freed Calles from prosecution
and allowed him to continue his presidential campaign without much
trouble. He became president of Mexico on December 1, 1924. However, many Villa supporters in congress continued believing that the
assassination had been ordered by a high office and pressed for further
investigation. Frustrated by the lack of effort to find the real culprit, in
January 1924, many Villistas, including his brother Hipolito, joined a
military coup to try to remove Obregon from power. Obregon managed
to suppress the rebellion and removed from government and military
positions any remaining Villista. Demands to find the real mastermind
stopped. Both Calles and Obregon lived the rest of their lives without
anyone being able to implicate them for this crime. Only in recent
years has enough evidence emerged to implicate them—too late for
justice. Anybody involved in the assassination was long dead.[19]

Trying to Rest in Peace

Villa found as little rest in death as he had in life. Villa's wish was to
be buried in Chihuahua where he had prepared a crypt, but Governor
Enriquez refused. Villa was, instead, unceremoniously buried in Par-

ral the day after his assassination. In 1926, a worker in the cemetery found Villa's grave opened. Someone had stolen his head. There has been great controversy about who did it, why it was done, and where the head is. Unfortunately, nobody knows for sure the answer to any of these questions.

Villa's contribution to the revolution was ignored by official history, but not by popular history. The revolutionary government that emerged from this decade of violence was composed of middle-class generals, led by Obregon and Calles, who had spent years fighting Villa. Thus, they tried to erase from history Villa's key role in the revolution while enhancing their own. However, in the minds of most Mexicans, Villa and Zapata remained the real heroes of the revolution. Villa's key role during the revolution received its first official recognition as late as 1976. Interested in increasing his own popular support, then President Luis Echeverria Alvarez tried to emphasize the popular origins of the revolution so he reinstated Villa and Zapata to their rightful place in the revolutionary pantheon. That year, on the anniversary of the revolution, a major military parade placed Villa's remains in the Monument to the Revolution in Mexico City. With high honors the headless body of Villa was placed between the remains of his friend Madero and his nemesis Carranza.

Francisco Villa remains a controversial figure, loved by those who see him as the Robin Hood of the revolution and despised by those who see him as a bloodthirsty bandit. While both images are accurate, the real Pancho Villa is a more complex figure than those simple white or black perceptions suggest. In any event, nobody can deny the central role that he played in the first social revolution of the 20th century.

Of course, it is impossible to know what the revolution would have been like if Pancho Villa had never joined it. There is no doubt, however, that militarily he was instrumental in defeating Porfirio Diaz and Victoriano Huerta, guaranteeing the elimination of the two last Mexican dictatorships. Politically, he inspired millions of Mexicans to refuse to submit to the powerful and to fight for their rights. Regardless of the ultimate political outcome of the revolution and the criticisms of his violent nature, Villa remains an inspiration for those Mexicans still affected by injustice in today's Mexico.

NOTES

1. Friedrich Katz, *The Life and Times of Pancho Villa* (Stanford, CA: Stanford University Press, 1998), 569.

2. Frank McLynn, *Villa and Zapata: A History of the Mexican Revolution* (New York: Carroll and Graf Publishers, 2000), 365.

3. Katz, *Life and Times of Pancho Villa*, 596.

4. Ibid., 609.

5. McLynn, *Villa and Zapata*, 369.

6. Paco Ignacio Taibo II, *Pancho Villa: Una biografía narrativa* (Mexico: Editorial Planeta, 2006), 680.

7. Katz, *Life and Times of Pancho Villa*, 628.

8. Ibid., 631.

9. Ibid., 633.

10. McLynn, *Villa and Zapata*, 378.

11. Katz, *Life and Times of Pancho Villa*, 715.

12. Ibid., 734.

13. Taibo, *Pancho Villa*, 747.

14. Katz, *Life and Times of Pancho Villa*, 756.

15. Ibid., 775.

16. Taibo, *Pancho Villa*, 808.

17. Katz, *Life and Times of Pancho Villa*, 772.

18. Ibid., 774.

19. Ibid., 775.

BIBLIOGRAPHY

Aguilar Camín, Héctor, and Lorenzo Meyer. *In the Shadow of the Mexican Revolution*. Translated by Luis Alberto Fierro. Austin: University of Texas Press, 1994.

Anderson, Mark Cronlund. *Pancho Villa's Revolution by Headlines*. Norman: University of Oklahoma Press, 2000.

Carroll, Bob. *Pancho Villa*. San Diego, CA: Lucent Books, 1996.

Caudet Yarza, Francisco. *Pancho Villa*. Madrid, Spain: Destin, 2003.

Cervantes, Federico. *Francisco Villa y la Revolución*. Mexico, DF: Instituto Nacional de Estudios Históricos de la Revolución Mexicana, 2000.

Dullers, John W. F. *Yesterday in Mexico: A Chronicle of the Revolution, 1919–1936*. Austin: University of Texas Press, 1961.

Englar, Mary. *Pancho Villa: Rebel of the Mexican Revolution*. Mankato, MN: Capstone Press, 2006.

Gómez Pérez, Marco Antonio. *Pancho Villa: El dorado de la revolución mexicana*. Mexico, DF: Grupo Editorial Tomo, 2002.

Gonzales, Michael J. *The Mexican Revolution, 1910–1940*. Albuquerque: The University of New Mexico Press, 2002.

Hurst, James W. *Pancho Villa and Black Jack Pershing: The Punitive Expedition in Mexico*. Westport, CT: Praeger, 2008.

Jaurrieta, José María. *Con Villa, 1916–1920: Memorias de campaña*. Mexico, DF: Consejo Nacional para la Cultura y las Artes, 1997.

Katz, Friedrich. *The Face of Pancho Villa: A History in Photographs and Words*. El Paso, TX: Cinco Puntos Press, 2007.

Katz, Friedrich. *The Life and Times of Pancho Villa*. Stanford, CA: Stanford University Press, 1998.

Katz, Friedrich. *Mexico Since Independence*. Edited by Leslie Bethell. New York: Oxford University Press, 1999.

Krauze, Enrique. *Mexico: Biography of Power*. Translated by Hank Heifetz. New York: Harper Collins, 1997.

Krauze, Enrique, and Margarita de Orellana. *Francisco Villa: Entre el ángel y el fierro*. Mexico, DF: Fondo de Cultura Económica, 1996.

Marcovitz, Hal. *Pancho Villa*. Philadelphia, PA: Chelsea House Publishers, 2003.

McLynn, Frank. *Villa and Zapata: A History of the Mexican Revolution*. New York: Carroll and Graf Publishers, 2000.

Morales, Fred M. *Francisco Villa*. El Paso, TX: El Paso/Juárez Historical Museum, 2006.

O'Brien, Steven, and Francisca González-Arias. *Pancho Villa*. New York, Chelsea House Publishers, 1995.

Plana, Manuel. *Pancho Villa and the Mexican Revolution*. New York: Interlink Books, 2002.

Sheina, Robert L. *Villa: Soldier of the Mexican Revolution*. Dulles, VA: Potomac Books, 2004.

Solares, Ignacio. *Columbus*. Mexico, DF: Santillana, S.A., 1998.

Stout, Joseph Allen. *Border Conflict: Villistas, Carrancistas, and the Punitive Expedition, 1915–1920*. Forth Worth: Texas Christian University Press, 1999.

Taibo, Paco Ignacio II. *Pancho Villa: Una biografía narrativa*. Mexico, DF: Editorial Planeta, 2006.

Villa, Guadalupe, and Rosa Helia Villa. *Pancho Villa: Retrato Autobiográfico 1894–1914*. Mexico, DF: Santillana Ediciones Generales, 2005.

Villegas, Cosio. *Historia General de Mexico*. Mexico: El Colegio de Mexico, 2009.

Welsome, Eileen. *The General and the Jaguar: Pershing's Hunt for Pancho Villa: A True Story of Revolution and Revenge*. Lincoln: University of Nebraska Press, 2007.

Womack, Jr., John. *Zapata and the Mexican Revolution*. New York: Vintage Books, 1970.

INDEX

About the Author

ALEJANDRO QUINTANA, Ph.D., is an assistant professor of history at St. John's University in New York City. He is the author of *Maximino Ávila Camacho and The One-Party State: The Taming of Caudillismo and Caciquismo in Post-Revolutionary Mexico*.